# EASTERN WASHINGTON AND OREGON In Bloom

# EASTERN WASHINGTON AND OREGON In Bloom

## Find and Identify the 150 Most Common Wildflowers

Ellen Kuhlmann and Mark Turner

Photography by Mark Turner

TIMBER PRESS
PORTLAND, OREGON

Frontispiece: Carey's balsamroot (*Balsamorhiza careyana*) in Waterworks Canyon west of Yakima, Washington


Cover photos by Mark Turner.



Timber Press
Workman Publishing
Hachette Book Group, Inc.
1290 Avenue of the Americas
New York, New York 10104

timberpress.com

Timber Press is an imprint of Workman Publishing, a division of Hachette Book Group, Inc. The Timber Press name and logo are registered trademarks of Hachette Book Group, Inc.

Printed in Dongguan, China, (TLF) on responsibly sourced paper

Text layout by Mary Velgos, based on series design by Hillary Caudle
Cover design by Leigh Kaisen

Endpaper illustration by Alan Bryan



ISBN 978-1-64326-369-4

A catalog record for this book is available from the Library of Congress.

# Contents

# Introducing Wildflowers

**Welcome!** This book, along with its companion volume, *Western Washington and Oregon in Bloom*, is designed to introduce you to some of the most common and showy native wildflowers in our region. Eastern Washington and Oregon have more in common with one another than they do with the west side of the states. We split the plants covered in this pair of books at the Cascade crest, the dividing line between the wetter west side and the dryer east side of the two states. The chapter on climate, geography, and habitat goes into more detail.

In this book we set out to include 150 species that are both representative of the region's larger flora and likely to be seen in accessible natural areas. We put a lot of time and thought into selecting the plants you'll find here, but considering that this number is only a small fraction of the thousands of native and nonnative wildflowers, trees, shrubs, and grasses that grow in our region, it's quite likely we had to leave out many of the flowers you'll encounter while you're hiking, camping, or otherwise exploring.

While most trees, shrubs, and grasses also produce flowers, this book focuses on what are commonly called wildflowers or forbs—species lacking woody tissue that have showy flowers. To determine which wildflowers to include, we used our personal knowledge gained from exploring the Northwest and its plants for more than thirty years. We also consulted herbarium records and iNaturalist reports. The final result is a worthy selection of the diverse native wildflowers of eastern Washington and Oregon.

## Getting to Know a Plant

It's easiest to identify plants when you adopt a systematic way of looking. While we're usually attracted first to the flowers and their shape and color, the rest of the plant is also important.

Start by getting an overall impression of the plant. Is it woody, like a tree or shrub? How big is it? Does it grow like a vine, form a mat on the ground, make a clump of stems, or have a single stem that stands by itself? Are the stems stiff and strong or are they flexible and slender? Are there any spines, prickles, or hairs?

Examine the leaves. Are they mostly right at the ground (basal) or do they grow along the stem? Some plants have both basal and stem leaves. What shape are the leaves? Leaf shapes are pictured inside the back cover. Stem leaves can be opposite each other or arranged alternately. Leaves can be attached to the stem with a stalk (called a petiole), clasp the stem, have little appendages at the attachment point (stipules), or appear to have the stem growing through the leaf. Many plants have compound leaves with several leaflets. You may need to count the leaflets and note how they're arranged. Leaf texture is another clue. Are they soft, leathery, hairy on one or both sides, or spiny?

Study the flowers. Identification usually requires a close look at the color, arrangement, and number of the flowering parts. Color is obvious, but it may change as the flowers age or among individuals of the same species. Sometimes petals have spots or blotches of a second color. Count the petals, if there are any. Some flowers don't have any petals, or they are very small and inconspicuous. Count the sepals, located at the base of the flower. For many plants, this will be enough to make an identification. However, you may also need to look closely to see how many stamens there are. Sometimes you need to see whether these sex parts are longer or shorter than the petals. For a few flowers, such as penstemons, you have to look closely to see how thick the hairs are inside and outside the flower. A 10x hand lens is useful for this close level of examination, can add a lot to your enjoyment of wildflowers, and doesn't weigh much in your pack. The visual glossary inside the front and back covers and the more extensive glossary beginning on page 377 can help you with technical terms you haven't yet learned.

Observe the habitat. Does the plant grow in the forest or out in the open? What is the soil like? What else is growing around your plant? Are you at the seashore, in the mountains, or somewhere in between? All of these are clues you can use to help you learn new plants.

## Organization

Flowers in this book are arranged first by flower color, then by family, genus, and species. This keeps related flowers of the same color together while helping introduce the important botanical concepts of how plants are related to each other but also unique in some way.

The fastest way to look up an unknown flower is to turn to the appropriate color section and then leaf through the pages until you find one that looks a lot like the plant in front of you. Then study the photographs closely and read the descriptions until you find a match. Use the maps to eliminate plants that don't grow where you are. You may find it helpful to read the descriptions a second time, perhaps with a friend who looks closely at the plant while you read. We couldn't avoid using some technical terms and it may take you some time to learn their meanings. The alternative was circumlocution, using many words to convey the meaning of a short, precise, but more technical word.

Because flower color can vary, you may not find a plant in the section where you expect it. Creamy whites are included with the white flowers, but pale yellows are with the darker yellows. Sometimes the distinction isn't very clear. Reddish purple flowers are with the reds but bluish purples are with the blues. Keep in mind that flower colors often vary within a species or change after pollination. For example, many lupines have a whitish area on the upper petal lip that turns reddish purple after pollination. You'll find it in the white section, not with the reds. Fern-leaved desert parsley, also known as chocolate tips, has either reddish brown or rich yellow flowers, with populations mostly containing plants of one color. We've placed it with the green and brown flowers. Those are just a few examples.

The index includes the common and Latin names for the plants described in the book. If you know a plant's name but aren't sure what it looks like, then turn to the index to find it quickly.

## Plant Names

Each plant species has a unique Latin name, which has two parts: the genus and the specific epithet. For a few plants, subspecies and varieties are listed, but for the most part this book sticks to identifying plants at the species level. Because plant names can change over time, generally due to additional DNA-based botanical research, we've listed Latin synonyms for some plants. The first name listed is the accepted name at the time of publication. We follow the

Washington Flora Checklist and the Oregon Flora Checklist. If they disagree, we evaluate the reasons why the names are different and use the one that we judge to be preferable for our purposes. The alternate names are usually older names that have been superseded but are still in common use or found in technical volumes that haven't been updated recently.

Each plant also has one or more common names. The same plant may be called by different names in different places, or the same name may refer to different plants in different places. Some plants have so many common names we couldn't list them all.

## Photographs

In most cases there is one photograph for each plant. They were selected to show as many of the important identifying characteristics as possible. Flowers receive more emphasis than foliage, which may appear somewhat soft-focus or in the background. Use the photographs to get a general feel for what the plant looks like, then read the description. Unfortunately, it is often impossible to show all pertinent characteristics in a single photograph.

## Maps

Each plant in this book has a map that shows the counties with records of the plant having been found there. The maps, which include adjacent areas in British Columbia and California, are based on plant collections housed at herbariums in the Northwest, along with records from iNaturalist. Herbaria contain collections of dried, pressed plants that have been identified and annotated by professional botanists. They are mostly housed at universities, although some national parks and other organizations have their own herbaria. iNaturalist collects observations from community scientists, with many of the observations confirmed by professionals. While we think the maps are pretty accurate as of publication, they should be used as a guide only, as you might find a plant in a county with no records of its occurrence, especially if it's been found in the surrounding counties.

## Descriptions

Each plant entry has several sections:

**Habitat** We use a few words to describe where the plant most commonly grows. If you're in a low-elevation environment and the description says the plant grows in mid-montane to alpine locations you probably need to look a little farther to find the right match. The chapter on climate and habitat can help you interpret the information in this section.

**Bloom** Most of our wildflowers bloom in spring or summer, with only a handful blooming in fall or late winter. The bloom seasons listed generally correspond to calendar seasons, but spring conditions can begin as early as February in warmer parts of our region. Some of our alpine plants bloom as soon as the snow melts, but that may not be until July, so they're listed as summer bloomers.

**Description** This section gives an overall picture of the plant, including its height and whether it's an annual, biennial, or perennial.

**Flowers** Flowers are generally described from the bottom up, which mostly means first describing bracts below the flower (if any), then sepals, and finally the petals (if any) and sex parts. Sometimes what looks like a petal is actually a sepal; we use "tepal" when these parts can't be easily classified as either sepals or petals.

**Leaves** Leaves are described from the base of the plant and then up the stem. When the leaves grow at the base of the plant, they're basal. Stem leaves can be arranged alternately on the stem, opposite each other, or in a circlelike whorl. Leaves can be either simple or compound, the latter meaning they're divided into multiple leaflets that can sometimes be confused with individual leaves.

**Fruit** Seeds are located within the fruit, but often they don't resemble the fleshy fruit you find at the grocery store. For example, many plants have a dry, one-seeded fruit that never opens to release the seed inside, called an achene. Sometimes the achene will have a feathery attachment (like dandelion fluff).

**Descriptive text** This section for each plant gives some interesting additional information such as how to distinguish from look-alike species.

# Exploring for Wildflowers

**Nearly everywhere you go,** even in the concrete jungle in the middle of big cities like Seattle, Portland, or Spokane, you'll find wildflowers (and likely nonnative weeds as well). In our region, with its winter-wet and summer-dry climate, most of our native flowers bloom in spring. As the flush of flowers wanes in the lowlands, the higher elevations burst into bloom with the snowmelt. There are a few species that bloom at lower elevations in summer, or bloom in fall, but they're the exceptions to the rule.

You'll find the highest concentration of wildflowers in open habitats such as meadows, the shrub-steppe, and along forest edges. Deep in the shade of our forests not enough sunlight reaches the ground for many flowers to grow and bloom, although a handful are adapted to this shady environment. Roadsides and the borders of hiking trails are often quite floriferous, sometimes with large populations of the same species. Flowers are generally picky about the conditions where they thrive, so you won't find all the plants in this book everywhere you go. The chapter on climate and habitat gives more information on plant environments.

## Access, Fees, and Permits

Wildflowers don't respect property boundaries; they grow wherever the conditions are right, regardless of whether their roots are sunk into public or private land. Many landowners are justifiably concerned about strangers wandering across their property, even if it's just to look at the flowers.

Ask permission before going onto private land. Remember to leave gates the way you found them and to walk softly.

Public lands are generally open to wildflower explorers, but entrance or parking fees may be required. These charges can change from year to year, and are not consistent from one state to another nor on public lands managed by different agencies. Before venturing out, it's worth checking with the relevant land-management agency to find out whether you'll be charged. The fees help maintain the parking areas and may also help with trail construction.

Private preserves, such as those owned by The Nature Conservancy or local conservation groups, also vary in their access restrictions. Usually there is no fee, but donations are gratefully accepted.

## Learning About Flowers

This book is an introduction to the wildflowers in our region. We kept the technical jargon to a minimum, but especially if you're new to botany you're sure to encounter some words you don't know. We used them because they more clearly describe the plants without getting overly wordy with convoluted circumlocutions. Over time, these terms will become more familiar. For now, use the glossary and the illustrations on the inside covers to get up to speed on the language.

We've placed the scientific name first with each plant description. While professional plant taxonomists have been busy updating our knowledge about how plants are related through DNA research and changing many scientific names in recent decades, there's still just one accepted scientific name for each species. That's not the case for common names. Some plants have multiple common names and some refer to more than one species, which can lead to confusion.

## Other Books and Apps

As your interest grows, you may want to further your knowledge with books that include more species. *Wildflowers of the Pacific Northwest* by Turner and Gustafson covers 1220 species and *Trees and Shrubs of the Pacific Northwest* by Turner and Kuhlmann includes 568 woody plants. Many people now look to plant apps for their smartphone. *Washington Wildflowers* and *Oregon Wildflowers*, both from High Country Apps, are comprehensive references for those states and were developed in cooperation with the plant professionals at the University of Washington and Oregon State University, respectively. They're not "point your camera at a plant and get an ID" apps but they include easy-to-use search tools. As your knowledge grows, you may ultimately decide one or more technical references are worth the investment.

Serious botanists rely on technical, dichotomous keys to definitively identify the plants they find. These books can be intimidating, but they go into much greater detail than is possible in a book like this one and allow for more definitive separation between similar species. Technical floras are heavy on specialized terminology and may call for you to use a hand lens to examine the flower parts or other small features to see distinguishing characteristics. Visit your library or a nearby herbarium to look up plants in these books before you invest in a copy.

There are three published floras for the region. Washington and Oregon as far south as Roseburg are covered in *Flora of the Pacific Northwest* by Hitchcock and Cronquist, which is updated and abbreviated from the five-volume *Vascular Plants of the Pacific Northwest*. The three-volume *Flora of Oregon* covers that state. Southern Oregon flora is more related to Northern California, so you might want to consult *The Jepson Manual: Vascular Plants of California*.

The "Going Further" chapter lists additional books you might want to consider as you expand your plant knowledge.

### Websites



Many websites have a wealth of information about native plants. In Washington, the Burke Herbarium Image Collection is a highly regarded reference. In Oregon, it's OregonFlora. USDA PLANTS covers the entire United States and has good distribution information. iNaturalist, available both on the web and as a smartphone app, is another good online tool. The Washington Native Plant Society website (wnps.org) has numerous plant descriptions and lists of plants found along many trails in the state. These lists can help you narrow down the choices when trying to determine what plant you've found.

You can also use your favorite search engine and enter the Latin name of the plant you want to learn more about as the search term. Like all web searches, there will be some irrelevant results, so you'll need to evaluate the source before deciding how reliable it is likely to be.

Field-trip participants gather around leader Abe Lloyd as he shows the difference between native and nonnative cranberries in a bog near Bellingham, Washington.

### Like-Minded Flower Explorers

It's more fun to go looking for flowers with other people who share your interest. There are native plant societies in both Washington and Oregon. Local chapters sponsor field trips to prime wildflower locations throughout the season and welcome nonmembers who want to learn more about their flora. You'll find announcements of these field trips on the organization's website. Search "native plant society" to find them.

Some other groups that lead plant hikes and field trips include parks and recreation departments, Sierra Club, The Mountaineers, and Audubon Society groups. Check the organization's website for information.



## Grow by the Inch, Die by the Foot

Sometimes we get so carried away with the excitement of finding new and interesting plants that we forget to pay attention to the impact we're making on their environment. You've heard the adage, "Take nothing but pictures and leave nothing but footprints." But often even our lightest footprints do significant damage. National Park rangers like to remind us that plants "die by the foot and grow by the inch." Our footsteps easily break delicate woody stems that take years to grow back, particularly in subalpine and alpine environments with short growing seasons. They compact the soil, reducing the air and water reaching roots, and they form social paths that other hikers follow.

A simple sign reminds hikers to stay on the trail.

You can minimize your impact by following Leave No Trace (LNT) principles. They're designed to protect wild lands, but LNT principles apply equally well in heavily traveled areas. They are (1) Plan ahead and prepare, (2) Travel and camp on durable surfaces, (3) Dispose of waste properly (pack it in, pack it out), (4) Leave what you find, (5) Minimize campfire impacts, (6) Respect wildlife, and (7) Be considerate of other visitors. Much information on LNT techniques is available at lnt.org.

Perhaps most important for the wildflower hunter is to travel on durable surfaces. You don't want to be responsible for destroying the very plants you've come to find and enjoy. If there is an established trail, stay on it. In some cases, as in heavily visited national parks, you absolutely must stay on established trails and rangers will remind you of the policy when they find you have strayed. You'll often find more examples of a plant that's a bit too far off the trail to examine just by hiking a little farther on.

In areas where there are no trails, you don't want to create a "user trail" that will encourage others to follow in your footsteps. Think about where you're walking and consider the consequences of your actions. Perhaps you can step from rock to rock. If not, grasses and sedges handle footsteps better than woody plants like heathers and huckleberries. When hiking with a group, practice "meadow walking." That means to spread out and hike side by side rather than follow the leader in a single-file line.

When you come to an interesting plant that you want to study, be aware of what you're trampling as you move around your subject. Be careful where you set your pack down. And when it's time for lunch, choose a rock, log, or grassy area to sit down.

With rare exceptions, you don't need to pick a flower to identify it. Leave the plant collecting to the professionals who have learned the techniques for preserving specimens and have received permission to collect from land managers.



## Safety

Searching for wildflowers is generally a low-risk activity, but there are hazards you should be aware of.

Rainy days can be a great time to explore for wildflowers, but dress for the weather like these participants on a Washington Native Plant Society field trip.

### Weather

What starts as a beautiful warm and sunny day can quickly turn cold, windy, and rainy, particularly in mountain environments. Dress appropriately for the conditions and be prepared for unexpected changes.

### Poisonous Plants

In some areas poison oak is thick. Learn to recognize its distinctive three leaves and woody stems. Some people are particularly sensitive to the rash-inducing chemicals in the leaves and stems. Poison ivy is similar, but much less common in our region. Stinging nettles are another

Poison oak (*Toxicodendron diversilobum*) in autumn with its characteristic three leaflets and white berries. All parts of the plant can cause an unpleasant skin reaction.

irritant to watch out for, although the effects don't last as long. Poison hemlock (page 61) is a common nonnative weed that is a significant skin irritant and deadly poisonous if eaten, even in small quantities.

### Rattlesnakes

Watch where you step and where you place your hands throughout the area east of the Cascades. Rattlesnakes will usually sound their distinctive warning rattle before you get too close, but you don't want to surprise or corner one. They're not particularly common and you're unlikely to see one of these generally shy reptiles but be cautious when you're in their territory.

### Ticks

Ticks are common in parts of our region, especially in tall grasses and weeds. They usually take several hours to attach themselves, so you have time to do a thorough tick check when you return to your car or home.

### Traffic

Many wildflowers grow at the side of roads, whether they're main highways or forest roads. Find a safe place to pull over and park, making sure you're out of the travel lane. Walk on the left, facing traffic. Stay well out of the road when examining the flowers. Even on lightly traveled forest roads you should expect vehicles to come by while you're stopped.

### Rockfall

You don't want to be either the cause or the victim of falling rock. Many areas with interesting flowers are on or near cliffs. Volcanic rock, our most common geologic formation, is often fractured and loose. Even on trails, it is easy to kick rocks down on the people hiking the switchbacks below you. If you do dislodge a rock, be sure to yell out "rock!" to alert anyone below you.

**Your Own Limits**

Know your limits—how far you can hike in a day and how much elevation you can climb (and descend). As you approach or exceed your limits, you're more likely to have an accident.



## Have Fun

Searching for and learning about our wildflowers is a lot of fun, whether you're a certified Hitchcock-carrying plant nut or a beginner. There's always a new plant to find or a new place to go. You can casually enjoy and learn about them as you go backpacking, kayaking, visiting historic sites, or go out intentionally searching for plants. There are enough flowers in the Northwest to keep you busy for years if you choose to try to find them all. Explore the trails through your neighborhood or travel to an exotic corner of the state. The choice is yours. But wherever you go, you're likely to find something in bloom if the season is right.

Glacier lilies (*Erythronium grandiflorum*), generate heat as they grow, melting the last vestiges of snow as they emerge and bloom.

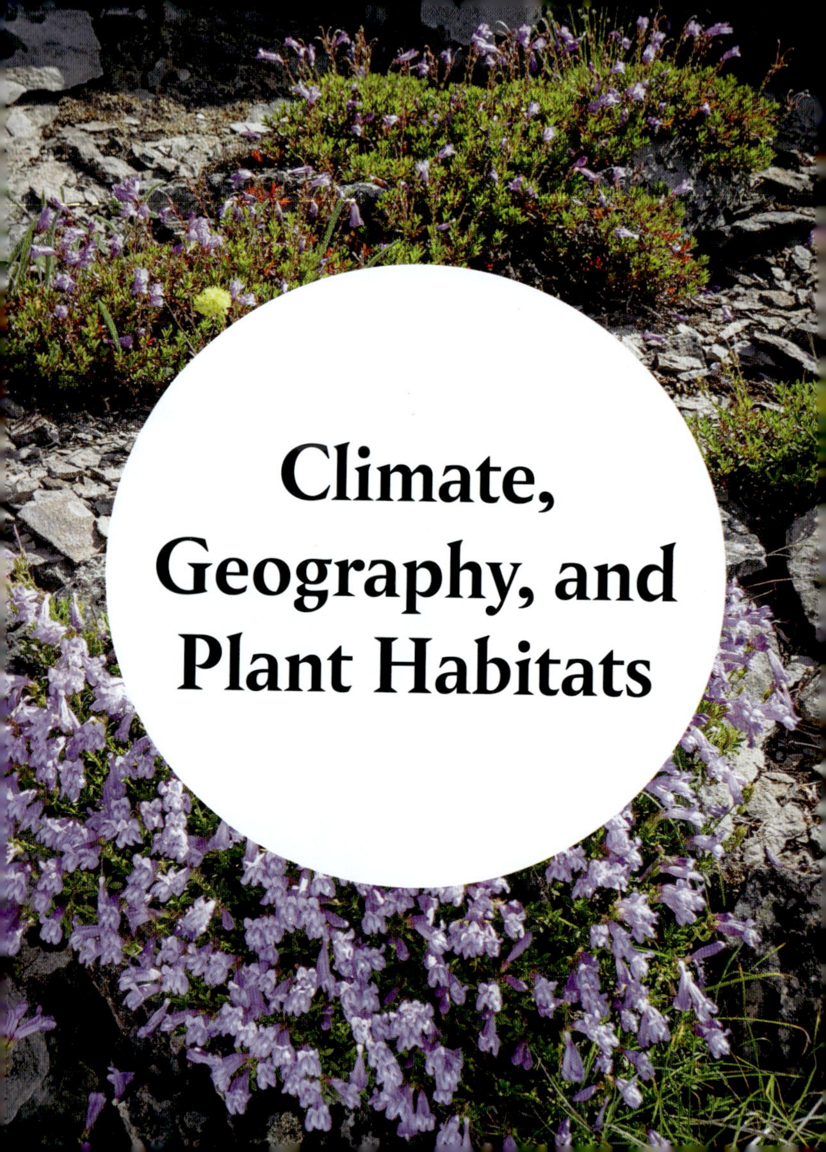

# Climate, Geography, and Plant Habitats

**Washington and Oregon** share similarities in climate, geography, and plant habitats. In broad terms, west of the Cascade crest gets the majority of its precipitation in winter, followed by dry but relatively cool summers. East of the mountains, precipitation still comes mainly in the winter months, but there's not as much of it and summers are considerably hotter. Both states have mountain ranges near the Pacific coast, a broad interior valley, the north-south Cascade Range, a wide relatively flat expanse east of the Cascades, and slopes that rise to the Rocky Mountains along their eastern borders.

However, we also have many localized microclimates and habitats that have major impacts on our flora. For example, Forks, on the Olympic coast in Washington, gets a whopping 116 inches of rain each year. In the Olympic rain shadow, Ebey's Landing on Whidbey Island receives only about 20 inches of rain. Mount Vernon, less than 40 miles to the northeast, averages 37 inches annually. Going another 50 miles east, Marblemount averages 83 inches of rain each year. East of the Cascades, Yakima and the Tri-Cities only get about 8 inches, but rainfall slowly increases as you head east to Spokane, which averages about 16 inches annually. Oregon has similar changes as one moves from the coast inland. Seaside gets 75 inches, Salem averages 38 inches, Bend gets about 12 inches, and Halfway, on the Idaho border, averages about 20 inches.

## Average Annual Precipitation (inches)

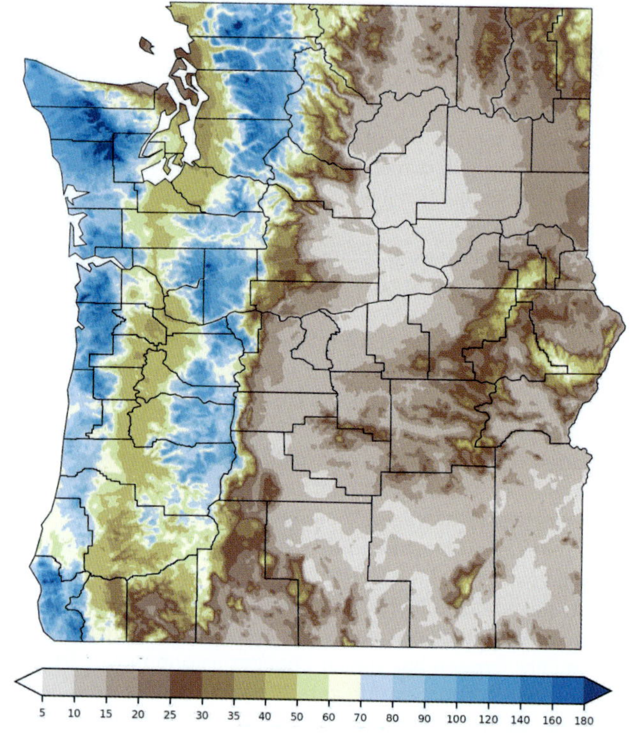


1981–2010 average annual precipitation for Washington and Oregon, mapped by the Western Regional Climate Center using data from the PRISM Climate Group at Oregon State University. Source maps available online at wrcc.dri.edu/Climate/prism_precip_maps.php

Our weather predominately originates over the Pacific Ocean and is strongly influenced by both the Coast and Cascade mountain ranges as it moves eastward. As rain clouds get pushed up against the mountains, they lose most of their moisture, leading to the dense green forests and fields on the west side and the dry sagebrush-steppe habitat common to the east. As the air moves farther east, it starts picking up moisture again, only to lose it again on the western slopes of the Rocky Mountains.

Most of our precipitation, on both sides of the mountains, comes in winter and in many areas much of it arrives as snow. When the jet stream swings north in summer, we experience weeks with little rain. Our weather, at least in the western lowlands where most of us live, is generally mild thanks to the moderating influence of the Pacific Ocean. Of course, east of the Cascades the oceanic influence is less and therefore the temperatures are more extreme. We also experience a north-south temperature gradient, with warmer summers in southern Oregon than northern Washington.

Elevation is also an important factor in plant habitats, affecting both temperature and precipitation. At higher elevations in the Olympics and the Cascades, deep winter snow usually lingers until mid-July. Mountain snowfall melts a bit earlier in the Klamath Mountains in southern Oregon and in the Wallowa Mountains, which don't get as much snow as the Cascades. The North Cascades have the largest number of glaciers in the lower 48 states, a long-term result of the heavy snowfall they experience most winters. However, as the earth has warmed over the past decades many of these glaciers are slowly disappearing, leaving U-shaped valleys in their wake.

With higher temperatures and less precipitation, the broad expanse of the Columbia Plateau can't support trees except in sheltered draws and riparian zones adjacent to waterways. Instead, sagebrush and other shrub communities predominate. In contrast, with mild winters and copious rainfall, western Washington and Oregon have extensive conifer forests with some of the world's largest trees.

Washington and Oregon have complex geology, which determines the soils derived from the underlying rocks. While large areas of both states are underlain by basalt and other volcanic rocks, there are also areas with sedimentary rocks like sandstone and limestone. And in a few areas, ultramafic rocks have been lifted from deep within the earth's crust to the surface. These ultramafic rocks are commonly called serpentine. You'll find serpentine primarily in the Klamath-Siskiyou Mountains in Oregon and in the Wenatchee Mountains in Washington. We also have areas of granite as our bedrock. All of these base rocks erode to different types of soil, and these soils influence which plants grow there. Serpentine-derived soils are infertile, with low levels of key minerals such as phosphorus and calcium and relatively high levels of magnesium, chromium, and nickel. Areas with serpentine soils often have a relatively large number of endemic plants that are able to tolerate or thrive in places that inhibit the growth of many species.

Soil depth is another factor influencing plant growth. Thin soils on rocky ridges support plants that have adapted to these conditions. Where soils are deeper and there's more moisture, faster-growing species crowd out the slow-growing ones. It's not so much that the plants that live in harsh conditions can't grow in better conditions as that they are often outcompeted. Challenging environments are often home to a greater diversity of plant species, while the resource-rich habitats tend toward more uniform and homogenous plant communities.

As a result of our summer-dry climate, most of our wildflowers bloom in spring and early summer both east and west of the Cascades. High in the mountains, many flowers emerge and bloom immediately after the snow melts. A few, like glacier and avalanche lilies, even generate enough heat from their bulbs to melt the last bit of snow and may bloom still surrounded by the white stuff. Wetland plants that are not water-limited often bloom in mid to late summer.

## Ecoregions

Ecoregions, which are a way to group areas considering the relationships of precipitation, geology, physiography, vegetation, climate, soils, land use, wildlife, and hydrology, are a convenient way to understand the ecology of an area at a high level. Mapping all of North America from Alaska to Mexico, there are three levels of ecoregions, with increasing levels of detail from the big-picture Level I to the more detailed Level III. In the conterminous United States, mapping has been extended to an even more detailed Level IV. The concept was first developed in the late 1970s for the US Forest Service. For our purposes, we'll be using the Level III ecoregions defined by the US Environmental Protection Agency in cooperation with agencies in Canada and Mexico (epa.gov/eco-research/ecoregions-north-america).

Within each ecoregion you can expect to find broadly similar growing conditions and thus a more predictable pattern of plant communities and plant types. Of course, hyperlocal conditions also play a big role. Examples include environmental factors such as aspect—whether you're on the north or south slope of a mountain; light—the full sun of a meadow or deep in the shade of a forest; and elevation—a valley bottom versus along a ridgetop.

## Ecoregions of Washington and Oregon

Washington and Oregon include all or parts of twelve ecoregions. We describe them here from north to south and west to east.

### Coast Range

The Coast Range includes most of the Olympic Peninsula in Washington (except the high mountains at the core of Olympic National Park) and continues down the west side of Oregon and into the northwest corner of California. It has a maritime climate with warm, mostly dry, summers and mild, very wet winters. Averaging 84 inches of annual precipitation, some areas get as much as 200 inches. All that rain

Old-growth western hemlocks (*Tsuga heterophylla*) along the Enchanted Valley Trail in Olympic National Park.

helps support dense coniferous forests, with Sitka spruce dominating along the coast and a mosaic of Douglas-fir, western hemlock, and western red cedar farther inland. Coast redwood is found in the far south of Oregon and in California. Much of the area has been heavily logged and replanted in Douglas-fir plantations. Larger communities in this ecoregion include Forks and Aberdeen, Washington; Astoria, Seaside, Tillamook, Newport, and Coos Bay, Oregon; and Crescent City and Eureka, California.

### Puget Lowland

The Puget Lowland ecoregion incorporates eastern Vancouver Island, and the Strait of Georgia lowlands in British Columbia, the lowlands around Puget Sound, and an area extending south to beyond Kelso, Washington. The climate is mild, with warm, dry summers and cool wet winters with

Profusion of spring wildflowers, including common camas (*Camassia quamash*), buttercups (*Ranunculus* spp.), field chickweed (*Cerastium arvense*), and harsh paintbrush (*Castilleja hispida*), on Yellow Island in Washington's San Juan Islands. Protected from development, Yellow Island is a Nature Conservancy preserve with limited public access.

occasional snow that usually melts quickly. There's a wide variation in annual rainfall, ranging from 12 inches in the Olympic rain shadow to 98 inches at higher elevations. While there are some low mountains, including the Chuckanuts south of Bellingham, most of the area is relatively flat to hilly. Relatively little undisturbed land remains in this highly urbanized region. Forests are dominated by Douglas-fir, western hemlock, grand fir, western red cedar, red alder, bigleaf maple, and a dense understory of species like salal, sword fern, Oregon-grape, and moss. Drier coastal areas often have Garry oak, shore pine, and Pacific madrone. Major population centers are Vancouver, Victoria, and Nanaimo, British Columbia; and Bellingham, Mount Vernon, Everett, Seattle, Tacoma, Olympia, and Centralia, Washington.

### Willamette Valley

The Willamette Valley lies between the Coast Range and the Cascades in Oregon. It's generally warmer than the similar Puget Lowland to the north, with warm and dry summers and mild, wet winters. Annual rainfall ranges from 35 to 63 inches, with the mountainous foothills on the east side of the valley getting the most. Once home to extensive native prairies, savannahs and forests, deciduous riparian forests, and seasonal wetlands, most of the Willamette Valley has been converted to agriculture. Natural areas feature Garry oak woodlands, prairies, and Douglas-fir or valley ponderosa pine woodlands. Riparian areas have black cottonwood, Oregon ash, bigleaf maple, alder, western red cedar, and a

Wet prairies like this one at Deer Creek Prairie Park near Sheridan, Oregon, were common before agriculture came to dominate the Willamette Valley. The purple flowers are common camas (*Camassia quamash*). This prairie had been converted to farmland and is undergoing restoration to preserve some rare plant species.

variety of shrubs. This gentle, rolling landscape is home to most of Oregon's population. Portland, Gresham, Beaverton, Hillsboro, Salem, Albany, Corvallis, Eugene, and Springfield are the major communities.





## Klamath Mountains

The Klamath Mountains are rugged and highly dissected with steep slopes, located south of the Willamette Valley and between the Coast Range and the Cascades in southwestern Oregon and adjacent California. Although the Mediterranean climate is generally mild, summers in the valleys can be quite warm with lengthy periods of drought, and relatively mild winters. The geology is complex and diverse, with sandstones and shales, granitic intrusive rocks, and substantial areas with ultramafic rocks (serpentine) and the unique plant

Western azaleas (*Rhododendron occidentale*) and Jeffrey pines (*Pinus jeffreyi*) at the edge of a fen at the Eight Dollar Mountain Botanical Trail near Selma, Oregon. California pitcher plants (*Darlingtonia californica*) are nearly hidden among the grasses and sedges in the foreground.

communities that grow there. Precipitation varies from 20 inches in the lower and dryer areas to 118 inches on the higher mountains, with much of that falling as winter snow. The Klamaths have the greatest conifer diversity of any place on the planet, but you'll also find tanoak, Garry oak, Pacific madrone, California black oak, chinkapin, and canyon live oaks here. Common conifers include Douglas-fir, white fir, incense cedar, Jeffrey pine, Shasta red fir, sugar pine, ponderosa pine, and western juniper. Larger communities include Roseburg, Grants Pass, Medford, and Ashland, Oregon; and Yreka and Weaverville, California.

**North Cascades**

The North Cascades include the northern end of the Cascade Range in northwest Washington and southern British Columbia, spanning both sides of the mountains between the Puget Lowland and the Columbia Plateau. This region also includes a disjunct area, the high Olympic Mountains at the core of Olympic National Park. Much of the area is national forest and national park lands. Climate here varies considerably, with temperate rainforest conditions at lower elevations in the west, a dry continental climate in the east, and deep winter snow and a short growing season in the high mountains in between. Summers are warm and dry; winters cool to cold and wet, with much of the precipitation coming as snow. The Mount Baker Ski Area set the record for the world's highest snowfall in one season during the winter of 1998–1999 with 1140 inches (95 feet) of snow. There are more glaciers here than in any other region of the United States outside of Alaska. Lower slopes on the west side are dominated by Douglas-fir, western hemlock, and western red cedar. Higher in the mountains you'll find Engelmann spruce, silver fir, subalpine fir, whitebark pine, and mountain hemlock.

Lewis's monkeyflowers (*Erythranthe lewisii*), cow parsnips (*Heracleum maximum*), and broadleaf lupines (*Lupinus latifolius*) fill a subalpine meadow along the Heliotrope Ridge Trail approaching Mount Baker.

Descending the slopes to the east, the forest transitions to Douglas-fir, ponderosa pine, and lodgepole pine. Larger communities include Concrete, Marblemount, Winthrop, Twisp, and Leavenworth, Washington.





### Cascades

The Cascades stretch from west-central Washington south through the spine of Oregon, and include a disjunct area in Northern California. The Cascades of Washington and Oregon are home to many volcanoes including Mount Rainier, Mount Adams, Mount Saint Helens, Mount Hood, Mount Jefferson, the Three Sisters, and Crater Lake, a caldera formed from the collapse of Mount Mazama. Large portions of this ecoregion are public lands. Summers are mostly dry and warm, with relatively mild to cool, very wet winters. Annual

Magenta paintbrush (*Castilleja parviflora* var. *oreopola*), broadleaf lupine (*Lupinus latifolius*), and numerous other species of wildflowers grow along a small stream in Cispus Basin in the Goat Rocks Wilderness near Packwood, Washington.

precipitation varies from 45 to 142 inches, depending on elevation and latitude with much of the higher-elevation precipitation coming as snow. Highly productive coniferous forests blanket most of the region, with Douglas-fir, western hemlock, western red cedar, bigleaf maple, and red alder at lower elevations. Higher up, Pacific silver fir, mountain hemlock, subalpine fir, noble fir, and lodgepole pine dominate. In the southern part of the region, you'll find Shasta red fir and white fir. The highest elevations have extensive subalpine meadows and rocky alpine zones. Few people live in this region; larger communities include Stevenson, Washington, and Cascade Locks and Oakridge, Oregon.

### Eastern Cascades Slopes and Foothills

The Eastern Cascades lie in the rain shadow of the Cascades region, running from central Washington to Northern California. The climate is more continental, with less precipitation and greater temperature extremes than in the mountains to the west. Summers are warm, bordering on hot, and dry, while winters are cold. Precipitation ranges from 20 to 138 inches, with the higher amount coming mostly as snow on the higher peaks. Historically, forests were somewhat open parkland with ponderosa and lodgepole pines, with shrub-steppe and grasslands dominating in the drier east. Vegetation is adapted to the dry continental climate, but is also highly susceptible to wildfire, especially after fire suppression over many decades led to a denser understory. The land has gently to steeply sloping mountains and high plateaus, interspersed with volcanic cones and some young lava flows. Like the Cascades and North Cascades, much of the land here is national forest or other public lands. Communities include Hood River, Bend, Klamath Falls, and Lakeview, Oregon.

Davidson's penstemon (*Penstemon davidsonii*) brightens a rocky outcrop on Black Butte near Bend, Oregon. Mount Jefferson is on the horizon.

### Columbia Plateau

The Columbia Plateau covers a huge portion of central and southeastern Washington and a wide band of northern Oregon south of the Columbia River between The Dalles and Pendleton. Underlain by thick layers of basalt, this region has dry, mid-latitude desert and steppe climates with hot, dry summers and cold winters. Precipitation comes mostly in winter, ranging from 6 inches in the rain shadow on the western edge to 23 inches in the northeast part of the region. Few trees grow here, except in the riparian zones along the Columbia River and its tributaries. Sagebrush, bitterbrush, and rabbitbrush are the taller shrubs, growing among a sea of grasses that include bluebunch wheatgrass, needle and thread, Sandberg bluegrass, and Idaho fescue. Invasive and extremely flammable cheatgrass has overtaken much of the region. Columnar basalt cliffs separating tablelands from the river valleys are common here, while other areas are covered by thick loess deposits. Irrigated agriculture is common, and in the rolling hills of the Palouse, dryland wheat and pulse crops dominate. Larger

Big sagebrush (*Artemisia tridentata*) among the basalt cliffs on the Seep Lakes Wildlife Management Area between Moses Lake and Othello, Washington.

population centers include Wenatchee, Ellensburg, Yakima, Richland, Kennewick, Pasco, Walla Walla, and Hermiston, Washington; and Pendleton and The Dalles, Oregon.





## Northern Rockies

The Northern Rockies, the product of continental crust uplift, encompass the northeast corner of Washington, along with adjacent areas of British Columbia, northern Idaho, and

Shrubby penstemon (*Penstemon fruticosus*), sticky cinquefoil (*Drymocallis glandulosa*), and big sagebrush (*Artemisia tridentata*) on a rock outcrop along the Kettle Crest Trail on the Colville National Forest east of Republic, Washington.

northwestern Montana. Somewhat surprisingly, there's some maritime influence here so the forests include many of the same species as wetter areas to the west—Douglas-fir, western and mountain hemlocks, western red cedar, and grand fir, along with ponderosa and lodgepole pines, western white pine, subalpine fir, and Engelmann spruce. The climate is somewhat severe, with relatively dry, warm summers and cold, snowy winters with moisture increasing from south to north. Precipitation ranges from 16 to 79 inches, with the greatest amount falling on the highest mountains. Larger communities include Spokane, Colville, Republic, and Newport, Washington.

### Blue Mountains

The Blue Mountains ecoregion covers much of northeastern Oregon and small portions of adjacent Washington and Idaho. Like the Cascades, but unlike the Northern Rockies, the Blue Mountains are mostly volcanic in origin, with only the high peaks of the Wallowa and Elkhorn mountains

A hiker passes Bonny Lake heading toward Aneroid Mountain in the Eagle Cap Wilderness.

consisting of intrusive rocks rising above the lava. The Blues are mostly lower and more open than other mountain ranges in the Northwest. The climate has both continental and Mediterranean influences, with warm, dry summers and cold winters. Precipitation ranges from 9 inches in the low valleys to 80 inches at high elevations, with much of that coming as winter snow. Low elevations contain mostly grasslands with bluebunch wheatgrass and Idaho fescue, sagebrush-steppe, and juniper woodlands. Forested areas have Douglas-fir, ponderosa pine, and grand fir at lower elevations; and subalpine fir, Engelmann spruce, whitebark and lodgepole pine up high, along with alpine meadows. Population centers include Madras, Redmond, Prineville, La Grande, Baker City, and Enterprise, Oregon.





### Snake River Plain

The Snake River Plain consists of plains and low hills centered on the Snake River that is incised into volcanic rocks.

Northern mule's ears (*Wyethia amplexicaulis*) in a meadow on the Pine Valley Ranch in Baker County, Oregon, with the Granite Mountains on the horizon.

Primarily in southern Idaho, a small part of this region extends into eastern Oregon between the Blue Mountains to the north and the Northern Basin and Range to the south. It is relatively flat, with warm, dry summers and cold winters. Rainfall is sparse, ranging from 4 to 25 inches. Similar to the Columbia Plateau, this region has a sagebrush-steppe environment with sagebrush, bluebunch wheatgrass, Idaho fescue, Indian ricegrass, rabbitbrush, and fourwing saltbush as dominant species. Irrigation water is abundant, so many of the alluvial valleys near the Snake River are agricultural. Most of the population centers are in Idaho: Boise, Nampa, Pocatello, Idaho Falls, and Twin Falls, as well as Ontario, Oregon.

**Northern Basin and Range**

The Northern Basin and Range ecoregion covers the southeast quarter of Oregon and adjacent areas of northern Nevada and southern Idaho. It is drier than the Columbia Plateau and generally higher in elevation, making it less suitable for agriculture. It's arid, with mid-latitude steppe and desert climates, characterized by hot summers and cold winters. Precipitation ranges from 6 inches at lower elevations to more than 39 inches on the upper reaches of Steens Mountain. Geologically mixed, the region has tablelands, dissected lava plains, scattered north-south trending mountains, and valleys with gently sloping alluvial fans. Several lakes and wetlands are stopover points for migrating waterfowl. Basins are dominated by sagebrush-steppe habitat with several species of sagebrush, rabbitbrush, scattered junipers, bluebunch wheatgrass, Idaho fescue, and Thurber's needlegrass. Ranges have mountain sagebrush, mountain-mahogany, juniper, and Idaho fescue at lower to mid-elevations, with Douglas-fir and aspen common higher up. Few people live here, with Burns, Oregon, the largest community. Christmas Valley, Jordan Valley, Frenchglen, and Burns Junction are much smaller populated places.

Sagebrush phlox (*Phlox aculeata*) growing up through sagebrush in the vicinity of Jordan Valley, Oregon.

## Habitats and Local Environments

Ecoregions describe broad areas with similar conditions, but if you've done any wandering about you've likely noticed that local environments play an important role in determining which plants grow there. For example, in the North Cascades ecoregion you'll find dense, relatively low-elevation forests, wetlands and other riparian zones, rocky balds, subalpine forests, and treeless alpine meadows. West- and south-facing slopes often support different plants than east- and north-facing ones. Within the Columbia Plateau, areas with thin and rocky soils support a surprisingly large assortment of plants, but they're not the same ones you'll find in places with a thicker soil layer.

The Pacific Northwest is generally a winter-wet, summer-dry environment. That means that most of our flowering plants put on their show in spring and early summer, before the soil dries out. In the mountains, places where snow lingers longer will have later-blooming flowers, often of the same species that might bloom earlier just a short distance away. The timing of the snowmelt is more important than calendar dates when looking for blooming wildflowers there.

Our coniferous forests have few wildflowers if the stand of trees is dense because not enough light reaches the forest floor. But within these dense forests are gaps that get more light—places where trees have fallen and opened the canopy, roadsides, edges of trails, and naturally occurring meadows. And some coniferous forests are more light-filled due to a lower tree density such as those on the eastern slopes of the Cascades that consequently have an abundance of spring wildflowers. Deciduous lowland forests, with their canopy of bigleaf maple, red alder, and black cottonwood, can have a profusion of early-season wildflowers that begin blooming before the trees have leafed out completely.

For each of the plants in this field guide we've used a few words to paint a picture of the habitats where you're most likely to find them. The habitat descriptions that follow cover both sides of the Cascades, even though this book focuses on just one side of the mountains. We hope that gives you a bigger picture of the habitat diversity here in the Northwest and might encourage you to explore the "other side of the mountains" if you haven't already.



### Forests

The mix of trees in Northwest forests, and the wildflowers at their feet, depends on the soil in which they sink their roots, the availability of water, and elevation, which can be seen as a proxy for temperature. Coastal and west-slope forests are much wetter than those dominated by the

Vanillaleaf (*Achlys triphylla*), lady ferns (*Athyrium filix-femina*), and sword ferns (*Polystichum munitum*) in the understory beneath old-growth Douglas-firs (*Pseudotsuga menziesii*) in the low-elevation westside forest at Rockport State Park, Washington.

Arrowleaf balsamroot (*Balsamorhiza sagittata*) and biscuitroots (*Lomatium* spp.) bloom under ponderosa pines (Pinus ponderosa) in an open eastside forest on the Okanogan-Wenatchee National Forest near Cashmere, Washington.

ponderosa and lodgepole pines found east of the Cascades. Lowland forests are found below about 1500 feet. Montane forests grow on the slopes of our mountains from roughly 1500 to 4000 feet, with lower montane forests often carpeted with a dense layer of mosses dotted with wildflowers in the more open places. Above 4000 feet the forest thins, becoming subalpine up to the treeline, above which is the treeless alpine zone. You'll find forests in most of our ecoregions, with the exceptions of the Columbia Plateau and Northern Basin and Range which are too dry to support trees except adjacent to streams.

### Alpine and Subalpine

Alpine and subalpine habitats are similar, the big difference being that true alpine areas are devoid of trees. In the subalpine, you'll find gradually thinning forests as you go higher, with pockets of trees dotting meadows and rocky slopes until you reach treeline. These are harsh environments,

Mountain arnica (*Arnica latifolia*) and broadleaf lupines (*Lupinus latifolia*) in an alpine meadow along the Ptarmigan Ridge trail approaching Mt. Baker.

with deep snow that lingers into mid-summer and a short growing season. South-facing slopes are often covered with dense flower-filled meadows, particularly where snowmelt water seeps into thicker soils. North-facing slopes, which melt out later, are more likely to have thin and rocky soils. Most plants in both the alpine and subalpine are perennials as establishing new plants from seed is challenging with the short growing season. Look for plants to bloom in these high-elevation areas soon after the snow melts, although there are some, like the gentians, grass-of-Parnassus, and asters, that bloom later in summer.

### Shrub-Steppe

The shrub-steppe habitat occurs in large areas of eastern Washington and Oregon. With little rainfall, the largest plants are shrubs like sagebrush, rabbitbrush, and bitterbrush. They're widely spaced, with native bunchgrasses (and non-native cheatgrass) and wildflowers between them. Within the

Rock buckwheat (*Eriogonum sphaerocephalum*) blooms among big sagebrush (*Artemisia tridentata*) and bitterbrush (*Purshia tridentata*) beneath the basalt cliffs of the Yakima River Canyon near the Umtanum Recreation Site in eastern Washington.

shrub-steppe are areas with deep loamy soils, sand dunes, and thin, rocky soil areas called lithosols. You'll also find basalt cliffs that have wildflowers growing in their cracks. In some areas there are vernal pools, places where winter rains accumulate and then slowly evaporate in spring, often with successive rings of wildflowers around their edges.

### Meadows and Prairies

Meadows and prairies are similar, with meadows generally smaller and at higher elevations. Prairies cover larger areas and often are drier or have thinner soils. The terms are sometimes used interchangeably. They're dominated by grasses, but often have profuse displays of wildflowers in spring. Both meadows and prairies can be wet or dry. Wet prairies are less common than they were before European settlers arrived and began draining them as they converted these bottomlands with rich soils to productive farmland, especially in Oregon's Willamette Valley. Mesic prairies have moderate moisture, being neither exceptionally wet nor dry.

Common camas (*Camassia quamash*) and western buttercups (*Ranunculus occidentalis*) blanket the mounded prairie at Mima Mounds Natural Area Preserve in Thurston County, Washington.

Broadleaf lupines (*Lupinus latifolius*), Sitka valerian (*Valeriana sitchensis*), and mountain arnica (*Arnica latifolia*) dominate the steep subalpine meadow below Excelsior Pass in the Mount Baker Wilderness near Glacier, Washington.

### Wetlands

Wetlands are areas where water covers the soil or is near the soil surface all or part of the year. These can be riparian, bordering streams, rivers, or lakeshores. They can also be isolated areas within forests, meadows, or prairies. Wetlands can be perennial like bogs, fens, and swamps. They can also be seasonal, wet in winter and spring but drying out after the rains stop in summer. By the time autumn rolls around, a seasonal wetland may look like it could be dry year-round.

Skunk cabbage (*Lysichiton americanus*) brightens a forest wetland on the outskirts of Bellingham, Washington.

## Coastal

Coastal habitats occupy a narrow strip of land adjacent to and near marine shorelines. Few plants grow directly on either rocky or sandy beaches that get inundated by salt water as the tide comes and goes. But at the back of the beach, you may find an assortment of grasses, sand verbena, beach morning glory, and other deep-rooted plants that help stabilize the shore. Some coastal areas have extensive undulating sand dunes, often with freshwater wetlands between drier forested areas. Dunes are most common on the Oregon coast between Florence and Coos Bay. Bluffs and headlands rise sharply from the coast, hosting wind-swept forests or dense shrub thickets.

Harsh paintbrush (*Castilleja hispida*) blooms on a grassy slope below the Deception Pass Bridge south of Anacortes, Washington.

### Rocky Areas

Rock underlies every habitat, with the type of rock determining the soil on top. In some places, there's just rock with very little exposed soil. These rocky areas include the basalt cliffs common in eastern Washington and Oregon, the lithosols interspersed in the shrub-steppe, as well as the talus and scree slopes found in the mountains as freezing and thawing gradually break them down. Alpine or subalpine rocky areas are very different from those of the Columbia Plateau, but what they have in common are plants that send their roots down through cracks to find nutrients and moisture while their aboveground parts are blasted by the sun and wind.

Lewis's monkeyflowers (*Erythranthe lewisii*) and red willowherb (*Chamaenerion latifolium*) bloom on a moist talus slope below Bearpaw Mountain on the Mount Baker–Snoqualmie National Forest near Glacier, Washington.

Desert yellow daisies (*Erigeron linearis*) grow at the base of basalt cliffs near Wanapum Dam, a few miles south of Vantage, Washington.

### Disturbed Areas

Disturbed areas include all the places where humans have changed the original natural habitat, as well as sites burned by naturally initiated wildfires or erosion. Road cuts, roadsides, farmland, vacant lots, clearcuts, and the edges of trails are all disturbed habitats. These areas are often dense with a diversity of plants, both native and nonnative. Many of our weeds, not included in this book, are particularly common in disturbed habitats.

Fireweed (*Chamaenerion angustifolium*) is among the first wildflowers to return following a forest fire. It's blooming here among burned lodgepole pines (*Pinus contorta*) along the Remmel Creek Trail in the Pasayten Wilderness north of Winthrop, Washington.

### Putting It Together

Many factors affect the mosaic of habitats across the Pacific Northwest. Rocks determine the soils above them, whether they're thick and loamy or thin and rocky. Rainfall and snow depth vary dramatically across the region. Elevation plays a big role, as do slope, aspect, and exposure to the sun. Ecoregions sketch a broad picture of the environment, while individual habitats paint a more detailed look. As you hike or drive backroads, you'll come to learn the plants in these individual habitats and discover that the same or similar habitat in other places is home to the same or similar group of plants. We're fortunate to live in a part of the continent with such diversity.

# White Flowers

Apiaceae—parsley family
*Conium maculatum*

# poison hemlock

**HABITAT** Roadsides, ditches, streambanks, meadows, lowland to mid-montane

**BLOOMS** Spring, summer

**DESCRIPTION** Toxic herbaceous biennial, nonnative, malodorous, taprooted, stems erect with purple blotches, leaves fernlike, inflorescence lacy, umbrella-like, with small flower clusters gathered into larger ones at the stem tip and leaf axils, plants 1½–10 ft. tall

**FLOWERS** Tiny, petals 5, white, spoon- to heart-shaped, tips notched, stamens 5, longer than the petals, styles 2

**LEAVES** Alternate, stalked, nonhairy, outline of the blade triangular, 6–12 in. long, divided 3–4 times, ultimate segments small, shiny green, tips pointed

**FRUIT** Dry, egg-shaped, ribs curved, 2-seeded

A decoction of poison hemlock, a highly poisonous invasive weed native to Europe, is thought to have been used to kill Socrates in ancient Greece. Native species western water-hemlock (*Cicuta douglasii*) is highly poisonous as well. Western water-hemlock has similar white umbrella-shaped flower clusters, but in contrast to poison hemlock, it is a perennial, has much larger, lance-shaped leaflets, and lacks purple stem blotches.

Apiaceae—parsley family
*Ligusticum grayi*

# Gray's lovage

**HABITAT** Forest openings, meadows, rocky areas, seeps, mid-montane to subalpine

**BLOOMS** Summer

**DESCRIPTION** Herbaceous perennial, taprooted, nonhairy, stems 1 to several, erect, leaves fernlike, inflorescence umbrella-shaped, lacy, rays of the umbel with flower cluster at the tips, plants 8–24 in. tall

**FLOWERS** Tiny, petals 5, white to pinkish, oblong to heart-shaped, tips notched, stamens 5, longer than the petals, styles 2

**LEAVES** Basal, stem leaves absent or few and alternate, stalked, blades pinnately divided 1–3 times, leaflets ½–1 in. long, lance- to egg-shaped, edges lobed, tips pointed

**FRUIT** Dry, 2-seeded, rounded, ribbed with a narrow, winged edge

Culinary lovage (*Levisticum officinale*), native to Iran and Afghanistan, is closely related to our native lovages (*Ligusticum* spp.). Gray's lovage can be mistaken for one of the desert parsleys (*Lomatium* spp.). One way to tell the two genera apart is by the fruit shape. Fruit of desert parsleys are flattened, while those of lovage are round.

Apiaceae—parsley family
*Lomatium macrocarpum*

# large-fruit desert parsley, giant-seed lomatium, large-fruited biscuitroot





**HABITAT** Shrub-steppe, often in serpentine soils, forest openings, lowland to higher montane

**BLOOMS** Spring

**DESCRIPTION** Aromatic herbaceous perennial, taprooted, stems branch at the base, spreading or upright, inflorescence umbrella-shaped, rays of the umbel tipped by a flower cluster, showy bracts below, plants 4–10 in. tall

**FLOWERS** Tiny, stalked, sepals absent, petals 5, white, purplish white, or yellow, stamens 5, styles 2, flowers bisexual or male

**LEAVES** Basal only or also alternate along the stem, stalked, blades grayish green, divided into linear, lobed leaflets, surfaces woolly-hairy or simply hairy

**FRUIT** Dry, 3-ribbed, to ¾ in. long, 2-seeded

Large-fruit desert parsley holds its stems upright or sprawling with the flower clusters near the soil. It is a long-lived perennial and may skip flowering for several years. Grazing decreases the abundance of large-fruit desert parsley while it increases after fire. Native Americans have traditionally collected the fleshy taproots to eat raw, boil, or dry for future use.

Asparagaceae—asparagus family
*Leucocrinum montanum*

# sand lily

**HABITAT** Sandy or rocky areas, shrub-steppe, dry forests, lower montane to mid-montane

**BLOOMS** Spring

**DESCRIPTION** Herbaceous perennial, ephemeral, rhizomatous with fibrous roots, stem absent, leaves basal, grasslike, flowers solitary, showy, fragrant, set among the leaves, plants 2–4 in. tall

**FLOWERS** Star-shaped, white, floral tube 2–3 in. long, tepals 6, oval to lance-shaped, ½–1 in. long, edges smooth, tips pointed, stamens 6

**LEAVES** Basal, tufted, blades linear, 3–8 in. long, spreading, edges smooth, tips pointed

**FRUIT** Capsule, egg-shaped, ¼ in. long, stored underground, few-seeded, seeds black

Not found in Washington, sand lily grows in eastern Oregon from Jefferson County south and east. Diminutive, with fragrant white flowers, sand lily is ephemeral with the aboveground plant parts dying back to ground level after flowering. Unusually, the capsular fruit is stored underground among the roots; the method of seed dispersal is unknown.

Asparagaceae—asparagus family
*Maianthemum stellatum*

# starry Solomon's seal, star-flowered Solomon's seal

**HABITAT** Mesic to dry forests, meadows, rocky slopes, streambanks, lowland to subalpine

**BLOOMS** Spring, summer

**DESCRIPTION** Herbaceous perennial, rhizomatous, patch-forming, stems erect, leafy, inflorescence an unbranched, few-flowered cluster at the stem tip, plants 6–24 in. tall

**FLOWERS** Star-shaped, fragrant, tepals 6, creamy white, oblong to lance-shaped, to ¼ in. long, stamens 6

**LEAVES** Alternate, stalk absent, blades flat to folded, oval to lance-shaped, 1–6 in. long, shiny green, edges smooth, tips pointed

**FRUIT** Berry, round, dark blue to reddish black, seeds 1–6

Starry Solomon's seal is found throughout Canada and most of the United States, except for the southern states. It grows on both sides of the Cascades in Washington and Oregon. The leaves of starry Solomon's seal are narrower and often folded in drier habitats and wider and unfolded in wetter areas. It grows well in garden settings; plant it in rich, well-drained soils in partial shade. The berries are edible, considered somewhat bitter and tart.

Asparagaceae—asparagus family
*Triteleia hyacinthina* (*Brodiaea hyacinthina*)

## white triteleia, white hyacinth, fool's onion

**HABITAT** Shrub-steppe, streambanks, vernal pools, meadows, lowland to middle elevations

**BLOOMS** Spring, summer

**DESCRIPTION** Herbaceous perennial from a bulb, short-hairy or nonhairy, stem 1, erect, grasslike, inflorescence a flat-topped cluster of stalked flowers at the stem tip, plants 1–2 ft. tall

**FLOWERS** Star-shaped, ¼–½ in. long, white with a greenish stripe or bluish white, rarely blue, tepals 6-lobed, lobes oblong, longer than the floral tube, stamens 6, pistil 1

**LEAVES** Basal only, 1–2, blades linear, 4–16 in. long, edges smooth, tips pointed

**FRUIT** Capsule, egg-shaped, seeds many, black

White triteleia has also been called fool's onion as the foliage resembles that of *Allium* species. Onions have tepals that are separate, while those of *Triteleia* spp. are joined at the base. White triteleia grows on both sides of the Cascades, ranging from British Columbia to California. It is commercially available and grows well in sunny gardens.

Asteraceae—aster family
*Achillea millefolium*

## common yarrow, milfoil





**HABITAT** Forest openings, fields, meadows, shrub-steppe, disturbed areas, lowland to alpine

**BLOOMS** Spring, summer, fall

**DESCRIPTION** Herbaceous perennial, aromatic, rhizomatous, stems erect, sparsely to densely hairy, leaves fernlike, inflorescence a branched, flat-topped cluster of heads at the stem tip, plants 1–2 ft. tall

**FLOWERS** Bracts of the head hairy, in overlapping shingled rows, both ray and disk flowers, rays white to pink, disk flowers creamy white

**LEAVES** Basal and alternate on the stem, sparsely to densely hairy, stalked except those of upper stem stalkless, blades 1–14 in. long, lance-shaped, pinnately divided, lobes linear, tips pointed

**FRUIT** Achene, nonhairy

Highly aromatic, common yarrow contains a number of volatile oils, tannins, and other compounds such as salicylic acid, the active ingredient in aspirin. It has a long history of use as a medicinal herb, made into poultices, salves, and teas. Yarrow grows well in garden settings but may spread aggressively if not contained. Circumboreal in distribution.

Asteraceae—aster family
*Antennaria dimorpha*

# low pussytoes, cushion pussytoes





**HABITAT** Shrub-steppe, open forests, rocky or sandy soil, lowland to middle elevations

**BLOOMS** Spring

**DESCRIPTION** Herbaceous mat-forming perennial, separate male- and female-flowered plants, root crown branched, stems many, inflorescence a solitary head at the stem tip, plants ½–4 in. tall

**FLOWERS** Bracts of the head in overlapping shingled rows, those on male heads about half as long as the bracts on female heads, rays absent, disk flowers whitish, female flowers longer than male flowers (photo shows male)

**LEAVES** Basal and alternate along the stem, linear to lance-shaped, grayish green, densely silky-hairy, edges smooth, tips pointed, to 1½ in. long

**FRUIT** Achene, hairy, tuft of hair at tip

Low pussytoes forms small clumps and prefers lithosol habitats. Stoloniferous pussytoes (*A. flagellaris*) looks similar to low pussytoes and grows in the same type of habitat, but has thin, arching runners (stolons) with a small leaf rosette at the end, while low pussytoes does not.

Asteraceae—aster family
*Chaenactis douglasii*

# dustymaidens, hoary false yarrow





**HABITAT** Shrub-steppe, forest openings, rocky areas, lowland to alpine

**BLOOMS** Spring, summer

**DESCRIPTION** Biennial or perennial, woolly-hairy, taprooted, stems 1 to several, erect, leaves fleshy, inflorescence a flat-topped cluster of stalked heads, plants 6–24 in. tall

**FLOWERS** Bracts of the head linear, glandular-hairy or simply glandular, tips pointed, all disk flowers, white, cream, pinkish white or pink, styles protruding from the petal tube

**LEAVES** Basal and alternate along the stem, stalked, blades pinnately divided into somewhat linear leaflets, these often again divided, grayish green or green, surfaces woolly-hairy, edges curled, tips often rounded, alpine plants lack basal leaves

**FRUIT** Achene, hairy or glandular-hairy, with tuft of hair at the top

Dustymaidens is adapted to arid habitats and rocky, often unstable soils. It frequently colonizes disturbed sites and is propagated for use in restoration projects for this reason. Dustymaidens grows well in sunny, dryland garden settings and is pollinated by bees.

Asteraceae—aster family
*Erigeron pumilus*

## shaggy fleabane, shaggy daisy

**HABITAT** Shrub-steppe, grasslands, dry forests, lowland to middle elevations

**BLOOMS** Spring, summer

**DESCRIPTION** Herbaceous perennial, taprooted, stems many, erect, branched, leafy, spreading-hairy, inflorescence of several stalked heads from the upper leaf axils or solitary at the stem tip, plants 2–12 in. tall

**FLOWERS** Bracts of the head in rows, linear to lance-shaped, spreading-hairy, glandular, tips pointed, both ray and disk flowers present, rays white, pink, or blue, to ½ in. long, disk flowers yellow

**LEAVES** Basal and alternate along the stem, blades linear to lance-shaped, spreading-hairy, ¾–3 in. long, edges smooth, tips pointed

**FRUIT** Achene, sparsely to moderately short-hairy, achene surface visible, with hair tuft at the top

Shaggy fleabane has a lengthy blooming period, is drought-tolerant, prefers sandy to gravelly soils, and attracts a variety of pollinators. Similar species cushion fleabane (*E. poliospermus* var. *poliospermus*) can be distinguished from shaggy fleabane by its densely hairy achenes and unbranched stems with solitary flowers.

Boraginaceae—borage family
*Cryptantha torreyana*

# Torrey's cryptantha





**HABITAT** Dry forests, shrub-steppe, open slopes and flats, lowland to mid-montane

**BLOOMS** Spring, summer

**DESCRIPTION** Annual, white stiff-hairy, taprooted, stems 1 to few, erect, branched or not, inflorescence usually 2 coiled clusters of stalkless flowers at the stem tip, sometimes from the leaf axils, coils straightening as the flowers bloom, plants 4–15½ in. tall

**FLOWERS** Tiny, sepals 5, lance-shaped, long stiff-hairy, tips pointed, petals white, tubular, 5-lobed, lobe tips rounded, not much longer than sepals

**LEAVES** Alternate along the stem and basal, blades linear to oblong, hairy, edges smooth, tips pointed, ¾–2 in. long, stalks absent

**FRUIT** Nutlet, 4 per flower, egg-shaped, smooth, shiny black

Torrey's cryptantha is widespread and commonly seen in dry habitats from late spring to summer. Identification of species in this genus relies heavily on nutlet characteristics. It is considered closely allied with basin cryptantha (*C. ambigua*), which has bumpy nutlets. Hybrids between the two species are known to occur.

Brassicaceae—mustard family
*Thelypodium laciniatum*

# cut-leaf thelypody, thick-leaf thelypody, feathery thelypodium

**HABITAT** Cliffs, rocky areas, shrub-steppe, low to high elevations

**BLOOMS** Spring, summer

**DESCRIPTION** Herbaceous biennial, nonhairy, taprooted, stems solid, erect, branched, flowers in spirelike clusters at the stem tip and from the leaf axils, plants 1–3 ft. tall

**FLOWERS** Vase-shaped, sepals 4, greenish white or purplish, tips rounded, petals 4, white or purple, linear, tips rounded, ¼–½ in. long, stamens 6, pistil 1

**LEAVES** Basal and alternate along the stem, with stalks to 4 in. long, blades lance- to egg-shaped, 3–9 in. long, edges lobed, wavy, or toothed, tips pointed

**FRUIT** Pod, 1–4½ in. long, stalked, spreading outward, curved or not, seeds many

Cut-leaf thelypody grows at the bottom of cliffs, on talus slopes, and rock outcrops within the shrub-steppe zone. It may be confused with similar species many-flowered thelypody (*T. milleflorum*), which has hollow stems, white sepals and petals, and pods that curve upward instead of spreading outward.

Caryophyllaceae—pink family
*Cerastium arvense*

## field chickweed, meadow chickweed

**HABITAT** Open slopes, meadows, forest openings, rocky areas, lowland to alpine

**BLOOMS** Spring, summer

**DESCRIPTION** Herbaceous perennial, usually hairy, taprooted or rhizomatous, stems creeping to erect, leafy, inflorescence an open, branched cluster at the stem tip, plants 2–12 in. tall

**FLOWERS** Saucer-shaped on slender stalks, sepals 5, lance-shaped, to ⅛ in. long, glandular-hairy, tips pointed, petals 5, heart-shaped, white, to ¼ in. long, tips rounded, stamens 10, styles 5

**LEAVES** Opposite, linear to lance-shaped, ¼–1 in. long, mostly hairy, edges smooth, tips pointed, often with smaller leaf bundle in the axil

**FRUIT** Capsule, oblong, curved to one side, seeds brown

Plants near the coast and at lower elevations are more densely hairy than montane specimens. Alpine chickweed (*C. beeringianum*), restricted to high elevations, looks much like field chickweed, but it lacks the smaller leaf bundles in the leaf axils, is densely hairy, and has wider, oblong leaves.

Caryophyllaceae—pink family

*Eremogone franklinii (Arenaria franklinii)*

## Franklin's sandwort, Thompson's sandwort

**HABITAT** Sand dunes, rocky areas, shrub-steppe, lowland to middle elevations

**BLOOMS** Spring

**DESCRIPTION** Subshrub, nonhairy, taprooted, stems many, trailing to erect, branched, leaves overlapping, inflorescence a dense several-flowered cluster at stem and branch tips, plants 1–6 in. tall

**FLOWERS** Star-shaped, sepals 5, lance-shaped, stiff, tips pointed, petals 5, lance- to spoon-shaped, white, tips rounded, slightly shorter than or longer than sepals, stamens 10

**LEAVES** Opposite, needlelike, stiff, bluish green, ¼–¾ in. long, edges smooth, tips sharp-pointed and spreading

**FRUIT** Capsule, nonhairy, seeds black

Franklin's sandwort thrives in sand dunes, sandy shrub-steppe, and rocky areas. Its leaves are stiff and needlelike, and persist, withered, at the base of the plant. Two varieties are recognized: var. *franklinii* has petals shorter than the sepals, and var. *thompsonii* has petals longer than the sepals. Variety *franklinii* is the predominant variety in Oregon and Washington, with var. *thompsonii* rare in Washington and suspected to be extirpated from Oregon.

Caryophyllaceae—pink family
*Moehringia macrophylla* (*Arenaria macrophylla*)

## large-leaf sandwort, big-leaved sandwort

**HABITAT** Forests, forest openings, balds, rocky slopes, lowland to mid-montane

**BLOOMS** Spring, summer

**DESCRIPTION** Herbaceous perennial, patch-forming, rhizomatous, stems erect to trailing, hairy, inflorescence an open, few-flowered cluster at the stem tip, plants 2–10 in. tall

**FLOWERS** Saucer-shaped, stalked, sepals 5, ovate to lance-shaped, surfaces short-hairy, tips pointed, petals 5, white, oblong, tips rounded, petals slightly shorter or longer than the sepals, stamens 10, pistil 1, styles 3

**LEAVES** Opposite, stalkless, oval to lance-shaped, 1–2 in. long, short-hairy, edges smooth, tips pointed, basal leaves absent

**FRUIT** Capsule, round to egg-shaped, seeds few

Large-leaf sandwort is characterized by its opposite, pointed leaves topped with delicate white flowers. It grows in shady dry to mesic forests, in forest edges or openings, and in balds and rocky areas. Bluntleaf sandwort (*M. lateriflora*) is similar to large-leaf sandwort but has rounded sepal tips, petals much longer than the sepals, and rounded leaf tips.

Caryophyllaceae—pink family
*Silene oregana*

# Oregon catchfly, Oregon campion

**HABITAT** Meadows, forest openings, rocky slopes, mid-montane to subalpine

**BLOOMS** Summer

**DESCRIPTION** Herbaceous perennial, taprooted, stems 2 to several, erect, upper stem glandular-hairy, leafy, flower clusters at the stem tip and from upper leaf axils, plants 1–1½ ft. tall

**FLOWERS** Bell-shaped, sepals 5-lobed, glandular-hairy, veins prominent, purplish, petals 5, white to pinkish white, 4-lobed, lobes divided into 6–10 unequal, fringelike segments, stamens 10, styles 3

**LEAVES** Basal and opposite along the stem, stalked, blades lance- to spoon-shaped, 1½–3 in. long, sparsely hairy, tips pointed or rounded, stem leaves smaller, sometimes stalkless, and glandular-hairy

**FRUIT** Capsule, oval, seeds numerous

The term catchfly refers to insects being "caught" by the sticky glandular hairs on the plant stem. Oregon catchfly can be separated from closely related species mountain catchfly (*S. bernardina*) as it has 4 petal lobes of equal length, rather than the unequally sized 6–10 lobes of Oregon catchfly.

Fabaceae—pea family
*Astragalus lentiginosus*

# freckled milkvetch, specklepod milkvetch





**HABITAT** Shrub-steppe, grasslands, open forests, lowland to subalpine

**BLOOMS** Spring, summer

**DESCRIPTION** Herbaceous perennial, short-hairy, taprooted, stems several, trailing with upturned tips or erect, leaves pealike, flowers stalked, in dense clusters from the leaf axils, plants 4–16 in. long or high

**FLOWERS** Two-lipped, to ½ in. long, white, pinkish, or purplish-tinged, upper lip larger than the lower, sepals tubular, 5-toothed, short-hairy, stamens 10

**LEAVES** Alternate along the stem and basal, stalked, pinnately divided into 11–19 leaflets, leaflets lance- to egg-shaped, ¼–½ in. long, tips rounded

**FRUIT** Pod, lance- or egg-shaped, hairy or not, often freckled or mottled

Freckled milkvetch can grow on disturbed sites and is tolerant of alkaline soils. Several varieties have been recognized, mainly delineated by flower size and pod shape. Milkvetch species are difficult to identify, and often both flowers and mature fruit are needed for definitive identification.

Fabaceae—pea family
*Astragalus whitneyi*

# balloon milkvetch, Whitney's locoweed

**HABITAT** Rocky areas, open forests, often on serpentine, mid-montane to alpine

**BLOOMS** Spring, summer

**DESCRIPTION** Herbaceous perennial, short-hairy, tap-rooted, stems several, trailing to erect, 2–12 in. long, leaves pealike, with a papery bract at the leaf axil, inflorescence a compact cluster of 5–20 stalked flowers at the stem tip

**FLOWERS** Two-lipped, yellowish white, often lavender-tinged, or pinkish purple, upper lip larger than the lower, tubular sepals hairy, 5-toothed, stamens 10

**LEAVES** Alternate, stalked, pinnately divided into 9–21 leaflets, leaflets lance- to egg-shaped, tips rounded or pointed

**FRUIT** Pod, ¾–2 in. long, inflated, egg-shaped, reddish- to purplish-mottled, drooping

The distinctive pod of balloon milkvetch is a good aid to identification. Similar species Cotton's milkvetch (*A. australis* var. *cottonii*), rare and endemic to the Olympic Mountains of Washington, can be distinguished by its smaller, to 1 in. long, oblong pods. Balloon milkvetch is found from Washington south to California, and east through Idaho and Nevada.

Hydrophyllaceae—waterleaf family
*Phacelia hastata*

## silverleaf phacelia, whiteleaf phacelia

**HABITAT** Rocky areas, shrub-steppe, forests, meadows, lowland to alpine

**BLOOMS** Spring, summer

**DESCRIPTION** Herbaceous perennial, hairy, taprooted, stems 1 to several, erect to trailing, foliage often silvery green, flowers in coiled clusters at the stem tip and from the upper leaf axils, plants 8–20 in. tall

**FLOWERS** Bell-shaped, stalked, sepals 5, lance-shaped, bristly-hairy, petals 5-lobed, white, yellowish white, lavender, or purple, lobes oblong to egg-shaped, tips rounded, stamens 5, protruding from the petals, pistil 1

**LEAVES** Basal and alternate on the stem, blades oval to lance-shaped, 1–5 in. long, veins prominent, short-hairy, edges smooth or lobed, tips pointed

**FRUIT** Capsule, egg-shaped, hairy, seeds 1–3

Silverleaf phacelia is a short-lived perennial that can colonize disturbed sites and is drought-tolerant. It has a lengthy bloom period and is visited by bees, moths, and butterflies. Silverleaf phacelia grows easily in gardens, reseeds readily, and is used in revegetating mines and roadsides.

Melanthiaceae—bunchflower family
*Toxicoscordion venenosum*
(*Zigadenus venenosus*)

## meadow death camas



**HABITAT** Meadows, forest openings, sagebrush-steppe, lowland to mid-montane

**BLOOMS** Spring

**DESCRIPTION** Ephemeral herbaceous perennial from an egg-shaped bulb, stem erect, leaves grasslike, flowers in a stalked, dense cluster at the stem tip, plants 6–24 in. tall, toxic

**FLOWERS** Saucer- to bell-shaped, white to cream, 6-lobed, lobes lance- to egg-shaped, the inner 3 longer than the rest, stamens 6, styles 3

**LEAVES** Basal and alternate along the stem, blades linear, 3–12 in. long, becoming bractlike near the stem tip

**FRUIT** Capsule, cylindric, seeds many, light brown

The bulb and leaves of meadow death camas are poisonous to humans and livestock. Vegetatively it looks similar to and often grows with common camas (*Camassia quamash*), which is edible. In bloom they are easily separated by flower size and color. It is common for Native American communities that collect camas bulbs to sometimes weed out meadow death camas within collecting areas to prevent accidental poisoning.

Melanthiaceae—bunchflower family
*Veratrum californicum*

## California false hellebore, California corn lily

**HABITAT** Meadows, streambanks, forest openings, lowland to subalpine

**BLOOMS** Summer

**DESCRIPTION** Herbaceous perennial, toxic, short-hairy, rhizomatous, stems 1 to several, stout, erect, unbranched, leafy, inflorescence a branched, 1–2 ft. long flower cluster at the stem tip, branches erect to spreading, plants 5–8 ft. tall

**FLOWERS** Star-shaped, tepals 6, white to greenish white, oval to lance-shaped, ¼–½ in. long, edges smooth to toothed, tips pointed or rounded, stamens 6, styles 3

**LEAVES** Alternate, blades lance- to egg-shaped, 8–12 in. long, ribbed, edges smooth, tips pointed

**FRUIT** Capsule, egg-shaped, nonhairy

Similar species green corn lily (*V. viride*) has green flowers, drooping inflorescence branches, and is not found at lower elevations. Siskiyou false hellebore (*V. insolitum*), rare in Washington but secure in Oregon, can be distinguished by its wider, egg-shaped tepals and hairy rather than nonhairy capsules. Although California false hellebore has striking foliage, its extreme toxicity when eaten by humans or other mammals should be considered before planting it.

Montiaceae—spring beauty family
*Claytonia perfoliata (Montia perfoliata)*

## miner's lettuce





**HABITAT** Rocky areas, forest openings, disturbed areas, lowland to mid-montane

**BLOOMS** Spring

**DESCRIPTION** Annual, taprooted, stems several, erect, green, inflorescence a narrow cluster of stalked flowers at the stem tip with a round cup-shaped leaf below, plants 2–14 in. tall

**FLOWERS** Saucer-shaped, sepals 2, oblong, petals 5, oblong, white to pinkish, to ¼ in. long, stamens 5, styles 3

**LEAVES** Basal leaves green, held erect, stalked, blades lance- to diamond-shaped, to 2 in. long, stem leaf a green cup-shaped disk below the inflorescence, ¼–4 in. across

**FRUIT** Capsule, seeds 1–3, shiny black, elaiosome present

Leaves of miner's lettuce are edible; the name originated with its use by miners as a salad green. It blooms while soils are moist in spring, then withers as soils dry and temperatures rise in summer. Similar species red miner's lettuce (*C. rubra*) can be distinguished by its reddish foliage and spreading, rather than upright basal leaves.

Onagraceae—evening primrose family
*Oenothera cespitosa*

## fragrant evening primrose, tufted evening primrose, stemless evening primrose

**HABITAT** Rocky slopes, sandy flats, shrub-steppe, lowland to middle elevations

**BLOOMS** Spring, summer

**DESCRIPTION** Herbaceous perennial, hairy or not, taprooted, stem short or absent, basal leaves many, inflorescence of several fragrant, showy flowers with long floral tubes, plants to 10 in. tall

**FLOWERS** Tubular with flared saucer-shaped lobes, white, fading to pink, sepals 4-lobed, lobes bent back, floral tube 1½–5½ in. long, 4-lobed, stamens 8, pistil 1

**LEAVES** Basal only, 4–10 in. long, stalked, blades lance- to spoon-shaped, edges toothed or smooth, tips pointed or rounded

**FRUIT** Capsule, oblong to egg-shaped, seeds numerous

Fragrant evening primrose grows in rocky, sandy, or clay soils. The flowers open in the evening and close at midday. Night-flying hawkmoths are one of the species' main pollinators, as the hawkmoths have a long proboscis that can reach the nectar at the bottom of the floral tube.

Onagraceae—evening primrose family
*Oenothera pallida*

# pale evening primrose, whitestem evening primrose

**HABITAT** Sand dunes, shrub-steppe, lower elevations

**BLOOMS** Spring, summer

**DESCRIPTION** Fragrant herbaceous perennial, clump-forming, hairy or not, taprooted with rhizomelike lateral roots, stems 1 to several, erect, whitish, flowers solitary in the leaf axils, plants 4–18 in. tall

**FLOWERS** Saucer-shaped, white with yellow at the base, fading to pink, sepals 4-lobed, floral tube ¾–1¼ in. long, 4-lobed, egg-shaped, ½–1 in. long, tips rounded or notched, stamens 8, pistil 1, stigmas 4-lobed

**LEAVES** Alternate, stalked, blades linear to lance-shaped, 1–2 in. long, edges wavy, toothed or not, tips pointed

**FRUIT** Capsule, linear, curved, seeds many

Pale evening primrose flowers open in the evening and close at midday. It is pollinated by long-tongued moths and bees. In eastern Oregon hairy evening primrose (*O. deltoides*) grows in similar habitats and can be distinguished by the often prostrate stems and egg-shaped leaves only near the stem tip.

Orchidaceae—orchid family
*Cypripedium montanum*

## mountain ladyslipper

**HABITAT** Forests, shrubfields, floodplains, lowland to high montane

**BLOOMS** Spring, summer

**DESCRIPTION** Herbaceous perennial, glandular-hairy, rhizomatous, stems 1 to several, erect, flowers 1–3 near stem tip, stalked, each with a leafy bract below, plants 8–27 in. tall

**FLOWERS** Slipper-shaped, petals 3, sepals 3, sepals and 2 petals lance-shaped, somewhat twisted, reddish brown, edges wavy, tips pointed, the 3rd petal pouched, slipperlike, white to purplish-tinged, stamens 3, 1 petal-like, yellow with reddish spots

**LEAVES** Alternate, glandular-hairy, stalkless, blades oval, clasping the stem, edges smooth, tips pointed, 2–6 in. long

**FRUIT** Capsule, oval, ribbed, seeds many

Mountain ladyslipper grows in small populations in full or partial shade, often found in forests with shrubby understories. It also grows in shrubfields and floodplains. Do not pick or collect them if you are fortunate enough to see it; mountain ladyslipper populations are easily decimated by collecting, and the plants usually do not survive transplanting.

Plantaginaceae—plantain family
*Penstemon deustus*

# hot-rock penstemon, hot-rock beardtongue

**HABITAT** Rocky areas, grasslands, shrub-steppe, meadows, lowland to mid-montane

**BLOOMS** Spring, summer

**DESCRIPTION** Subshrub, clump-forming, taprooted, stems few to many, erect, unbranched, flowers arranged in loose, tiered clusters at the stem tip and from upper leaf axils, plants 8–24 in. tall

**FLOWERS** Two-lipped, glandular-hairy, sepals 5-lobed, lobes egg- to lance-shaped, petal tube narrow, upper lip 2-lobed, the lower 3-lobed, white and purple-lined, yellowish white, or lavender-tinged, ¼–¾ in. long, stamens 5, 1 sterile

**LEAVES** Opposite, sometimes whorled, stalked or not, blades egg- to spoon-shaped, ¼–2 in. long, surfaces hairy or not, edges toothed, tips rounded or pointed

**FRUIT** Capsule, seeds many

Mainly grows on volcanic substrates, but is occasionally found on limestone. It has four recognized varieties with one, variable hot-rock penstemon (*P. deustus* var. *variabilis*), rare and endemic to Washington and Oregon—it has narrow, often whorled leaves with few-toothed or smooth edges, while other varieties have strictly opposite leaves.

Plantaginaceae—plantain family
*Plantago patagonica*

## woolly plantain, Indian-wheat, Patagonia plantain

**HABITAT** Grasslands, sand dunes, shrub-steppe, forest openings, disturbed areas, lowland to middle elevations

**BLOOMS** Spring, summer

**DESCRIPTION** Annual, white woolly-hairy, taprooted, stems 1 to several, leaves basal only, grayish green, flowers in narrow, oblong clusters at the stem tips, plants 2–8 in. tall

**FLOWERS** Cross-shaped, tiny, sepals 4, oblong, woolly-hairy, petals tubular, 4-lobed, white to brownish, lobes egg-shaped, stamens 4, with bract below

**LEAVES** Basal, stalked, blades linear to lance-shaped, 1–5 in. long, surfaces woolly-hairy, tips pointed

**FRUIT** Capsule, 2-seeded

Woolly plantain ranges from Canada throughout most of the continental United States and south into Mexico. It is also found at the southern tip of South America, source of the species name *patagonica*. Although its flowers are small, the plant is quite attractive due to its grayish green foliage and the copious woolly hairs. Woolly plantain flowers are autogamous, meaning the flowers are self-fertilizing.

Polemoniaceae—phlox family
*Phlox hoodii*

# Hood's phlox, spiny phlox, cushion phlox





**HABITAT** Rock outcrops, shrub-steppe, rocky slopes, lowland to middle elevations

**BLOOMS** Spring

**DESCRIPTION** Herbaceous perennial, hairy, mat-forming, taprooted, stems many, erect, branched, leaves needlelike, flowers solitary at stem and branch tips, plants 1–4 in. tall

**FLOWERS** Trumpet-shaped, sepals 5-lobed, lobes linear, cobwebby-hairy, tips pointed, petals tubular, 5-lobed, white, pink, or lavender, lobes oval, sepals shorter than petal tube, stamens 5, pistil 1

**LEAVES** Opposite, blades linear, to ½ in. long, edges cobwebby-hairy, tips pointed, stalk absent

**FRUIT** Capsule, oval, seeds few

Hood's phlox typically grows in lithosol shrub-steppe communities, although it is also found in sandy areas and sometimes deeper-soiled shrub-steppe. It forms short mounds averaging 2–12 in. across, adding colorful patches of white to lavender across open slopes when in bloom. Hood's phlox is pollinated by butterflies, moths, and bees. Add it to rock or pollinator gardens where it grows best in full sun and rocky, well-drained soils.

Polygonaceae—buckwheat family
*Eriogonum elatum*

# tall buckwheat





**HABITAT** Shrub-steppe, forest openings, gravelly or sandy flats, ridges, lowland to mid-montane

**BLOOMS** Summer

**DESCRIPTION** Sturdy subshrub, taprooted, stems 1 to several, erect, branched, leafless, inflorescence at the stem tip, flat-topped, clusters few-flowered, with bell-shaped bracts below, plants 1–2½ ft. tall

**FLOWERS** Cup-shaped, tepals 6, white to cream, egg-shaped, hairy on the lower half, tips rounded, few flowers per bell-shaped bract, stamens 9

**LEAVES** Basal only, stalked, blades lance- to egg-shaped, 1½–6 in. long, sparsely hairy, green, edges smooth, tips pointed

**FRUIT** Achene, nonhairy

Summer bloomers like tall buckwheat provide important forage for butterflies and bees. Distinguish it from the somewhat similar bare-stem buckwheat (*E. nudum*) by the latter's smaller, ¼–2 in. long, oblong leaves that are white woolly-hairy beneath and its many flowers per cluster.

Polygonaceae—buckwheat family
*Eriogonum heracleoides*

## parsnip-flowered buckwheat, creamy eriogonum, Wyeth's buckwheat





**HABITAT** Shrub-steppe, dry forest openings, rock outcrops, lowland to subalpine

**BLOOMS** Spring, summer

**DESCRIPTION** Subshrub or herbaceous perennial, woolly-hairy, taproot woody, stems erect to trailing, clump-forming, flowering stems with 1 set of whorled leaves or none, inflorescence at the stem tip, flat-topped, clusters round, compact, with bell-shaped bracts below, plants 4–15 in. tall

**FLOWERS** Cup-shaped, tepals 6, white, cream, or pinkish, spatula- to egg-shaped, nonhairy, tips rounded, stamens 9

**LEAVES** Basal and whorled on the stem, stalked, blades linear to lance-shaped, 1–4 in. long, both surfaces grayish green, woolly-hairy, edges smooth, tips pointed

**FRUIT** Achene, hairy only on the upper portion

Parsnip-flowered buckwheat is somewhat similar to arrowleaf buckwheat (*E. compositum*) but has narrower leaves, lacks yellow flowers, and tends to grow on cooler sites. It makes a nice addition to a dryland pollinator or rock garden, thriving in sun or shade.

Polygonaceae—buckwheat family
*Eriogonum niveum*

# snow buckwheat

**HABITAT** Shrub-steppe, dry forests, sand dunes, bluffs, rock outcrops, lowland to middle elevations

**BLOOMS** Summer, fall

**DESCRIPTION** Subshrub or herbaceous, grayish green, clump-forming, taprooted, stems 1 to many, trailing to erect, branched, woolly-hairy, inflorescence open, leafy-branched clusters with tubular bracts below, plants 8–24 in. tall

**FLOWERS** Cup-shaped, tepals 6, white to pinkish, oval to egg-shaped, tips rounded, nonhairy, the outer 3 tepals wider than inner 3, few-flowered per tubular bract

**LEAVES** Basal and whorled at the branch nodes, stalked, blades oval, lance-, or egg-shaped, ¼–2 in. long, densely woolly-hairy, grayish green, edges smooth, tips rounded or pointed

**FRUIT** Achene, nonhairy

Snow buckwheat has long-lasting flowers that bloom from summer into fall, providing insects and other animals with late-season forage. It grows well in dryland wildlife or rock gardens, preferring sandy to rocky soils, and does not become weedy. It is highly drought-tolerant and often used to revegetate disturbed areas.

Polygonaceae—buckwheat family
*Eriogonum strictum*

## Blue Mountain buckwheat, strict buckwheat

**HABITAT** Shrub-steppe, rocky slopes, dry forests, lowland to subalpine

**BLOOMS** Spring, summer

**DESCRIPTION** Subshrub or herbaceous, grayish green, taprooted, stems 1 to several, trailing to erect, woolly-hairy, leaves mostly basal, flower clusters either open and much-branched or narrow and few-branched, plants 4–20 in. tall

**FLOWERS** Cup-shaped, 6-lobed, nonhairy, yellow, pink, or white, lobes oblong to egg-shaped, the outer 3 tepals wider than the inner 3, stamens 9

**LEAVES** Basal, long-stalked, blades oval to egg-shaped, ¼–1 in. long, surfaces both densely woolly-hairy or the topside less so, tips rounded or pointed

**FRUIT** Achene, nonhairy

*Eriogonum* species are called buckwheats due to their resemblance to culinary buckwheat (*Fagopyrum esculentum*). The inflorescences of Blue Mountain buckwheat can either have many branches each tipped with a small cluster or are little branched with larger, ball-shaped flower clusters. It does well in rock gardens and is considered a slow grower.

Santalaceae—sandalwood family
*Comandra umbellata*

# bastard toadflax





**HABITAT** Shrub-steppe, sandy to rocky slopes, ridges, lowland to subalpine

**BLOOMS** Spring, summer

**DESCRIPTION** Herbaceous perennial, nonhairy, rhizomatous, stems several, erect, flower clusters branched and compact at the stem tip and from upper leaf axils, plants 2–12 in. tall

**FLOWERS** Funnel-shaped, small, to ¼ in. long, petals absent, sepals tubular, 5-lobed, lobes lance-shaped, greenish white to purplish, tips pointed, stamens 5

**LEAVES** Alternate, fleshy, grayish green, blades oval to lance-shaped, to 1½ in. long, edges smooth, tips pointed

**FRUIT** Berrylike, blue to purplish brown, 1-seeded

Bastard toadflax is a hemiparasite, photosynthesizing but also connecting to roots of neighboring plants to obtain nutrients. It is a generalist, known to siphon nutrients from many different plant species. The berries are eaten by wildlife but not recommended for human consumption.

Saxifragaceae—saxifrage family
*Heuchera cylindrica*

# roundleaf alumroot, poker heuchera

**HABITAT** Rocky slopes, crevices, cliffs, lower montane to subalpine

**BLOOMS** Spring, summer

**DESCRIPTION** Herbaceous perennial, rhizomatous, stems 1 to several, erect, glandular-hairy, leafless, inflorescence a dense, cylindric flower cluster at the stem tip, plants 6–36 in. tall

**FLOWERS** Bell-shaped, sepals cream-colored, may be rose-tinged, sepal lobes 5, lance- to egg-shaped, glandular-hairy, tips pointed, petals absent or 1–5, linear, white, much shorter than the sepals, stamens 5

**LEAVES** Basal, stalks hairy or not, blades heart- to egg-shaped, nonhairy or glandular-hairy, lobes 5–7, shallow, edges toothed, tips rounded or pointed, stem leaves absent

**FRUIT** Capsule, seeds many

Mounds of basal leaves paired with erect stems topped by cream-colored flowers make roundleaf alumroot an attractive addition to native plant gardens. It is available through the nursery trade and grows well in dry, well-drained soils in sun to partial shade. Cultivars of alumroot are often called coral bells.

# Yellow Flowers

Apiaceae—parsley family
*Lomatium nudicaule*

## barestem biscuitroot, barestem desert parsley, pestle lomatium

**HABITAT** Grassy slopes, meadows, shrub-steppe, dry forests, lowland to mid-montane

**BLOOMS** Spring

**DESCRIPTION** Aromatic herbaceous perennial, nonhairy, taprooted, foliage bluish green, stems 1 to several, erect, inflorescence umbrella-shaped, rays of the umbel unequal, each ray with a cluster of small flowers at the tip, plants 8–36 in. tall

**FLOWERS** Tiny, stalked, sepals absent, petals 5, yellow, stamens 5, styles 2, bisexual or male only

**LEAVES** Mostly basal, stalked, blades pinnately divided 1–3 times, leaflets oblong to egg-shaped, 1–3½ in. long

**FRUIT** Dry, oblong to oval, ribbed with a winged edge, 2-seeded

Barestem biscuitroot is a long-lived perennial that tolerates disturbances like fire, resprouting afterward from the root system. It provides forage for wildlife and hosts larvae of several butterfly species. It was believed that barestem biscuitroot was pollinated by many types of insects, but recent research has shown that its primary pollinators are solitary, ground-nesting mining bees in the *Andrenidae* family.

Apiaceae—parsley family
*Lomatium triternatum*

## nineleaf biscuitroot, nineleaf lomatium, Lewis's lomatium

**HABITAT** Shrub-steppe, grassy slopes, dry forests, rocky areas, lowland to mid-montane

**BLOOMS** Spring

**DESCRIPTION** Aromatic herbaceous perennial, short-hairy, taprooted, stems 1 to few, erect, inflorescence umbrella-shaped, rays of the umbel unequal in length, each tipped with a cluster of small flowers, plants 8–30 in. tall

**FLOWERS** Tiny, sepals absent, petals 5, yellow, stamens 5, styles 2, bisexual or male only

**LEAVES** Basal and alternate on the stem, stalked, blades alternate, divided 2–3 times, leaflets linear, unequal in length, ½–4 in. long

**FRUIT** Dry, oval, nonhairy, ribbed with a winged edge, 2-seeded

Taproots of nineleaf biscuitroot store nutrients and water and can be several feet long. After the seeds mature, the aboveground parts wither, minimizing water loss during the hot, dry summer. Nineleaf biscuitroot is often utilized for dryland restoration. The term biscuitroot comes from the practice of turning the starchy taproot into the flour used to make biscuits.

Apiaceae—parsley family
*Osmorhiza occidentalis*

## western sweet-cicely

**HABITAT** Forests, open slopes, streambanks, lowland to mid-montane

**BLOOMS** Spring, summer

**DESCRIPTION** Aromatic herbaceous perennial, root system quickly splitting into many thin, fibrous roots, stems several, erect, branched, sparsely hairy or not, inflorescence umbrella-shaped, rays of the umbel with clusters of tiny flowers at the tips, plants 1–4 ft. tall

**FLOWERS** Saucer-shaped, tiny, sepals absent, petals 5, yellow or greenish yellow, oblong to egg-shaped, stamens 5, styles 2

**LEAVES** Basal and alternate along the stem, stalked, blades divided 1–3 times in three parts, leaflets lance- to egg-shaped, ¾–4 in. long, edges toothed or sometimes lobed, tips pointed

**FRUIT** Dry, linear to oblong, nonhairy, ¼–¾ in. long, 2-seeded

The roots, foliage, and seeds of western sweet-cicely have a licorice-like smell and taste. Native Americans have traditionally used it for culinary and medicinal purposes, brewing the roots into teas and using the leaves and seeds for flavoring food. Its name likely comes from the similar European sweet cicely (*Myrrhis odorata*).

Asteraceae—aster family
*Agoseris grandiflora*

# large-flowered agoseris, giant mountain dandelion





**HABITAT** Prairies, open forests, grassy slopes, lowland to mid-montane

**BLOOMS** Spring, summer

**DESCRIPTION** Herbaceous perennial with milky-white sap, sparsely hairy, taprooted, stems 1 to several, erect, leafless, head solitary at the stem tip, plants 1–2 ft. tall

**FLOWERS** Bracts of the head in several rows, the outer usually shorter and wider than the inner bracts, all ray flowers, rays strap-shaped, yellow

**LEAVES** Basal only, linear to lance-shaped, hairy, 4–15 in. long, edges smooth or lobed, if lobed then lobes linear to lance-shaped, oriented sideways or upward, tips pointed

**FRUIT** Achene, tapering to a beak 2–4 times longer than the achene body, topped with a tuft of hair

Large-flowered agoseris is a short-lived, colonizing species with wind-dispersed seeds that easily germinate on burned or otherwise disturbed soils. Similar species spear-leaved agoseris (*A. retrorsa*) can be distinguished as its leaf lobes point downward while those of large-flowered agoseris point up or outward.

Asteraceae—aster family
*Arnica cordifolia*

## heart-leaf arnica, heart-leaf leopardbane





**HABITAT** Forests, roadsides, meadows, lowlands to subalpine

**BLOOMS** Spring, summer

**DESCRIPTION** Herbaceous perennial, rhizomatous, stems 1 to few, erect, hairy, stem leaves 2–4 pairs, inflorescence usually a solitary head at the stem tip, plants 4–24 in. tall

**FLOWERS** Bracts of the head lance-shaped, ½–¾ in. high, spreading-hairy, sometimes glandular, both ray and disk flowers, rays yellow, oblong, to 1 in. long, disk flowers yellow

**LEAVES** Opposite on the stem, stalked to stalkless near the stem tip, blades heart-shaped except the top pair usually egg-shaped, 1½–4½ in. long, surfaces hairy, edges toothed, tips pointed, basal leaves similar to the stem leaves

**FRUIT** Achene, short-hairy, sometimes glandular, with hair tuft at the tip

Heart-leaf arnica can be confused with mountain arnica (*A. latifolia*), which grows in cool, moist montane habitats. Mountain arnica has oval to lance-shaped leaves, usually has 3 smaller heads per stem, and achenes that are fully or partly nonhairy.

Asteraceae—aster family
*Artemisia tridentata*

# big sagebrush

**HABITAT** Shrub-steppe, open forest, talus slopes, lowlands to subalpine

**BLOOMS** Summer, fall

**DESCRIPTION** Aromatic shrub, taprooted, stems erect, branched, bark grayish brown, leaves evergreen and deciduous, inflorescence a branched, open cluster of unstalked heads at the branch tips, plants 1–6 ft. tall

**FLOWERS** Bracts of the head short, lance-shaped, in shingled rows, densely hairy, all disk flowers, 3–8 per head, yellow

**LEAVES** Alternate, evergreen and deciduous, grayish green, densely short-hairy, wedge-shaped with 3 rounded teeth at the tip, ½–1 in. long

**FRUIT** Achene, hairy or not

Big sagebrush is variable in its morphology, with several recognized subspecies. It is not tolerant of alkaline soils or lithosol habitats. It provides many important functions to wildlife species including as forage, cover, and nesting sites. Several species are dependent on sagebrush, including the rare sage grouse, pygmy rabbit, sagebrush sparrow, and the pygmy short-horned lizard.

Asteraceae—aster family
*Balsamorhiza careyana*

# Carey's balsamroot

**HABITAT** Open slopes, shrub-steppe, grasslands, low elevations to mid-montane

**BLOOMS** Spring

**DESCRIPTION** Herbaceous perennial, hairy, taprooted, stems several, leaves green, flowers clustered in sunflower-like heads, 2–6 at the stem tip, plants 8–36 in. tall

**FLOWERS** Bracts of the head oblong, linear, or lance-shaped, hairy, both ray and disk flowers present, rays yellow, oblong to oval, disk flowers yellow

**LEAVES** Basal and alternate on the stem, stalked, basal blades triangular with a rounded base, 6–12 in. long, green, short-hairy with a sandpapery texture, edges smooth, wavy, or round-toothed, tips pointed, stem leaves few, much smaller and narrower than the basal leaves

**FRUIT** Achene, hairy or not

Carey's balsamroot is endemic to eastern Washington and Oregon and prefers dry habitats with fairly deep soils. It is usually found in drier habitats than those of arrowleaf balsamroot (*B. sagittata*). Balsamroots hybridize freely when their populations grow close together, the hybrids exhibiting a mix of characteristics from the parent species.

Asteraceae—aster family
*Balsamorhiza hookeri*

# Hooker's balsamroot, hairy balsamroot





**HABITAT** Shrub-steppe, rocky areas, forest openings, lowland to middle elevations

**BLOOMS** Spring

**DESCRIPTION** Herbaceous perennial, hairy, taprooted, basal leaves fernlike, stems erect to leaning, inflorescence a solitary sunflower-like head at the stem tip, plants 4–12 in. tall

**FLOWERS** Bracts of the head lance- to egg-shaped, hairy, both ray and disk flowers present, rays yellow, oval to egg-shaped, ¼–1¼ in. long, disk flowers yellow

**LEAVES** Basal, stalked, hairy, blades lance-shaped, 4–15½ in. long, grayish green, pinnately divided into many leaflets, leaflets again divided or lobed, stem leaves few

**FRUIT** Achene, nonhairy

Hooker's balsamroot grows on sites with a thin soil layer. The degree of hairiness differs significantly among populations of the species. Hispid balsamroot (*B. hispidula*), is a closely related species that has bright green rather than grayish green leaves, found in Oregon but not known from Washington. Hooker's balsamroot is known to form hybrids with other balsamroot species, notably with arrowleaf balsamroot.

Asteraceae—aster family
*Balsamorhiza sagittata*

## arrowleaf balsamroot

**HABITAT** Dry forests, shrub-steppe, meadows, lowland to mid-montane

**BLOOMS** Spring, summer

**DESCRIPTION** Herbaceous perennial, hairy, taprooted, all leaves basal, grayish green, stems many, inflorescence a single, stalked sunflower-like head at the stem tip, plants 8–30 in. tall

**FLOWERS** Bracts of the head linear to lance-shaped, woolly-hairy, both ray and disk flowers present, rays yellow, oval to lance-shaped, to 1½ in. long, disk flowers yellow

**LEAVES** Basal, stalked, blades arrowhead-shaped, 3–12 in. long, grayish green, densely soft-hairy, edges smooth to wavy, tips pointed

**FRUIT** Achene, nonhairy

Distinguish arrowleaf balsamroot from the similar Carey's balsamroot (*B. careyana*) by checking the number of sunflower-like heads per stem: arrowleaf balsamroot has 1, while Carey's balsamroot has 2 or more. A long-lived plant, arrowleaf balsamroot has a woody taproot that may be up to 4 in. across and 9 ft. deep with lateral roots spreading 3 ft. away from the main root. It is drought-tolerant, resprouts after fire, and prefers deep soils.

Asteraceae—aster family
*Cacaliopsis nardosmia (Luina nardosmia)*

# silvercrown luina, cut leaf cacaliopsis





**HABITAT** Forest openings, grassy slopes, meadows, lowland to mid-montane

**BLOOMS** Spring, summer

**DESCRIPTION** Herbaceous perennial, rhizomatous, stem usually 1, erect, basal leaves prominent, inflorescence a rounded cluster of stalked heads, plants 1–3 ft. tall

**FLOWERS** Bracts of the head in a single row, linear to lance-shaped, all disk flowers, yellow

**LEAVES** Alternate along the stem and basal, stalked, to 8 in. long and wide, round to kidney-shaped, deeply lobed, lobe edges sharp-toothed, upper stem leaves much smaller

**FRUIT** Achene, nonhairy, with tuft of white hair at the top

Silvercrown luina has a distinctive form, a tall flowering stem above large basal leaves. It is often found in partial shade and in clumps due to its rhizomatous habit. The basal leaves bear some resemblance to those of arctic sweet coltsfoot (*Petasites frigidus*), however coltsfoot leaves are bristle-tipped, while those of silvercrown luina are not.

Asteraceae—aster family
*Crepis atribarba*

## slender hawksbeard

**HABITAT** Shrub-steppe, dry forests, open slopes, lowland to mid-montane

**BLOOMS** Spring, summer

**DESCRIPTION** Herbaceous perennial, sparsely to woolly-hairy, exudes milky juice when cut, taprooted, stems 1–2, erect, branched, inflorescence an open cluster of stalked heads at the stem tip, plants 6–24 in. tall

**FLOWERS** Inner bracts of the head lance-shaped, grayish-hairy, often with black stiff hairs as well, tips pointed, outer bracts much shorter, all ray flowers, rays strap-shaped, yellow, tips toothed

**LEAVES** Basal and alternate along the stem, basal and lower stem leaves stalked, 4–13 in. long, blades divided into linear to narrowly lance-shaped leaflets, leaflet edges smooth or toothed, tips pointed, upper stem leaves not divided, linear

**FRUIT** Achene, greenish, with tuft of white hair at the tip

There are several hawksbeard species that grow in similar habitats as slender hawksbeard. The leaves of slender hawksbeard, with their narrow, spreading leaflets, are a reliable characteristic to distinguish it from other *Crepis* species.

Asteraceae—aster family
*Crocidium multicaule*

## gold stars, common spring-gold, gold fields

**HABITAT** Shrub-steppe, forest openings, rock outcrops, lowland to middle elevations

**BLOOMS** Spring

**DESCRIPTION** Annual, taprooted, stems 1 to several, erect, inflorescence a solitary head at the stem tip, plants 1–6 in. tall

**FLOWERS** Bracts of the head oval to egg-shaped, tips pointed, both ray and disk flowers present, rays yellow, oval to oblong, tips pointed, disk flowers yellow

**LEAVES** Alternate along the stem and basal, basal leaves stalked, blades lance-shaped, to 1 in. long, edges smooth or toothed, tips pointed, stem leaves linear, woolly-hairy in the axils

**FRUIT** Achene, hairy

Gold stars is a tiny beauty, often found in profusion early in the growing season. It prefers sandy to rocky soils within sagebrush (*Artemisia* spp.) or Garry oak (*Quercus garryana*) communities. It is the only species in the *Crocidium* genus. The name *Crocidium* comes from the Greek word *kroke*, meaning loose thread or wool, a reference to the woolly hairs in the leaf axils.

Asteraceae—aster family
*Ericameria nauseosa* (*Chrysothamnus nauseosus*)

## gray rabbitbrush, rubber rabbitbrush





**HABITAT** Shrub-steppe, sand dunes, rocky areas, lowland to mid-montane

**BLOOMS** Summer, fall

**DESCRIPTION** Deciduous shrub with a rounded shape, taprooted, stems branched, flexible, velvety hairy, flower heads in rounded or flat-topped clusters at the branch tips, plants $1\frac{2}{3}$–$6\frac{1}{2}$ ft. tall

**FLOWERS** Bracts of the head in several rows, inner rows longer than the outer, to ½ in. high, rays absent, disk flowers yellow

**LEAVES** Alternate, blades linear to lance-shaped, 1–3 in. long, grayish green or green, densely to sparsely hairy, edges smooth, tips pointed

**FRUIT** Achene, usually hairy, with hair tuft at the top

Gray rabbitbrush tolerates disturbance, resprouting following fire and often increasing in abundance in overgrazed areas. It is used in dryland restoration as it grows quickly, has deep roots, and does well in poor soils. Gray rabbitbrush flowers are an important food source for pollinators and other insects as it blooms later in the growing season.

Asteraceae—aster family
*Erigeron linearis*

# desert yellow daisy, lineleaf fleabane, linear-leaved daisy

**HABITAT** Shrub-steppe, rocky areas, lowland to middle elevations

**BLOOMS** Spring, summer

**DESCRIPTION** Herbaceous perennial, green to grayish, taprooted, stems many, erect, appressed stiff-hairy, leaves mostly basal, flower heads solitary at the stem tip, plants 2–8 in. tall

**FLOWERS** Bracts of the head in rows, oval, appressed-hairy, tips pointed, both ray and disk flowers, rays bright yellow, pale yellow, or cream, to ¼ in. long, disk flowers yellow

**LEAVES** Basal and alternate along the stem, blades linear, appressed stiff-hairy, ½–3½ in. long, edges smooth, tips pointed

**FRUIT** Achene, sparsely hairy, with hair tuft at the top

Two other yellow-rayed *Erigeron* species grow in similar habitats as desert yellow daisy. Piper's fleabane (*E. piperianus*) has bracts and leaf edges with spreading hairs and is endemic to Washington. Dwarf yellow fleabane (*E. chrysopsidis*) has leaf blades and bracts with spreading hairs. It grows in Washington near the Oregon border and in eastern Oregon.

Asteraceae—aster family
*Eriophyllum lanatum*

## Oregon sunshine, woolly sunflower, woolly yellow daisy

**HABITAT** Rocky areas, meadows, forest openings, lowland to subalpine

**BLOOMS** Spring, summer

**DESCRIPTION** Herbaceous perennial, woolly-hairy, taprooted, stems several, erect to trailing, inflorescence a solitary head at the stem tip, plants 4–24 in. tall

**FLOWERS** Bracts of the head lance- to egg-shaped, in one row, erect, woolly-hairy, both ray and disk flowers present, rays oval, yellow to golden yellow, ¼–¾ in. long, disk flowers yellow

**LEAVES** Alternate or opposite, blades lance-shaped, grayish green, divided into leaflets or not, woolly-hairy, ¼–3 in. long

**FRUIT** Achene, hairy or not, sometimes glandular

A variable species, Oregon sunshine is adapted to dry, sunny habitats. It has dense woolly hair on its foliage that traps water vapor close to the surface, thus reducing water loss through transpiration. Oregon sunshine grows well in rock or dry meadow gardens, spreads easily, and attracts a variety of pollinators. Plant it in sandy to rocky well-drained soil in sunny spots.

Asteraceae—aster family
*Gaillardia aristata*

# blanket flower, brown-eyed Susan

**HABITAT** Shrub-steppe, sandy flats, dry forests, lowland to mid-montane

**BLOOMS** Spring, summer

**DESCRIPTION** Herbaceous perennial, hairy, taprooted, stems 1 to several, erect, branches few to none, heads solitary or few at the stem tip, plants 8–27 in. tall

**FLOWERS** Bracts of the head in rows, lance-shaped, hairy, both ray and disk flowers present, rays yellow or reddish, often purplish-tinged, fan-shaped, ¼–1 in. long, tips 3-lobed, disk flowers reddish brown, rarely yellow, densely woolly-hairy

**LEAVES** Alternate, stalked, blades lance- or egg-shaped, 2–6 in. long, hairy, tips pointed, basal leaves absent or not

**FRUIT** Achene, densely hairy, with tuft of hair at the top

Blanket flower is drought-tolerant and prefers well-drained soils. It is utilized in wildland restoration and grows well in dryland gardens. Cultivars of blanket flower have been developed by the horticulture trade. Wildlife browse on its flowers and leaves and many insects shelter within it and gather pollen and nectar.

Asteraceae—aster family
*Helianthella uniflora*

# Douglas' helianthella, false sunflower

**HABITAT** Forest openings, meadows, rocky areas, lowland to mid-montane

**BLOOMS** Spring, summer

**DESCRIPTION** Herbaceous perennial, taprooted, stems 1 to many, erect, short-hairy, inflorescence a solitary sunflower-like head at the stem tip, plants 8–36 in. tall

**FLOWERS** Bracts of the head linear to lance-shaped, hairy, tips pointed, both ray and disk flowers present, rays oval, bright yellow, 1–1½ in. long, disk flowers yellow

**LEAVES** Opposite except may be alternate near stem tip, stalks absent, blades oval to lance-shaped, short-hairy, 4½–10 in. long, edges smooth, tips pointed, basal leaves wither early

**FRUIT** Achene, hairy, with 2 long bristles at the tip

Douglas' helianthella brightens open forests, meadows, and rocky areas with its sunflower-like blooms. Closely related to true sunflowers (*Helianthus* spp.), distinguish between the genera by looking at the achenes. *Helianthella* spp. achenes have 2 persistent bristles, while the achene bristles of true sunflowers easily detach from the fruit body.

Asteraceae—aster family
*Hieracium scouleri*

## Scouler's hawkweed, hound's-tongue hawkweed, western hawkweed

**HABITAT** Forest openings, open slopes, shrub-steppe, disturbed areas, lowland to mid-montane

**BLOOMS** Summer

**DESCRIPTION** Herbaceous perennial with milky juice, short-rhizomatous, stems 1 to few, nonhairy to densely long-hairy, inflorescence 1 to several heads in branched, open clusters near the stem tip, plants 1–2 ft. tall

**FLOWERS** Bracts of the head linear to lance-shaped, with glandular and nonglandular often blackish hairs, all ray flowers, bright yellow, strap-shaped

**LEAVES** Basal and alternate along the stem, 2–8 in. long, stalked or not, blades oval to lance-shaped, stiff-hairy, leaves much smaller on upper stem

**FRUIT** Achene, ribbed, with tuft of hair at the top

A helpful tip for recognizing hawkweeds is to look at the rays. Hawkweeds have rays with a squared-off edge with several teeth. As currently described, Scouler's hawkweed includes the formerly recognized taxa *H. cynoglossoides* and *H. albertinum*. Most hawkweeds have yellow flowers; only one in our area does not—white-flowered hawkweed (*H. albiflorum*).

Asteraceae—aster family
*Nestotus stenophyllus* (*Stenotus stenophyllus*, *Haplopappus stenophyllus*)

## narrowleaf goldenweed

**HABITAT** Shrub-steppe, rocky slopes, ridgetops, middle to high elevations

**BLOOMS** Spring, summer

**DESCRIPTION** Subshrub, taprooted, mat-forming, stems many, erect, leaves crowded near the base, inflorescence a solitary head at the stem tip, plants 1–4½ in. tall

**FLOWERS** Bracts of the head oval to lance-shaped, of similar lengths, glandular-hairy, tips pointed, both ray and disk flowers present, rays oblong, yellow, ¼ in. long, disk flowers yellow

**LEAVES** Alternate, blades linear, to ¾ in. long, surfaces glandular-hairy, edges hairy, tips pointed

**FRUIT** Achene, hairy, with a tuft of bristly hair at the top

Narrowleaf goldenweed prefers granitic or basaltic soils and is typically found in lithosol shrub-steppe communities. It is found in eastern Washington and Oregon, south to California and east into Nevada and Idaho.

Asteraceae—aster family
*Nothocalais troximoides* (*Microseris troximoides*, *Scorzonella troximoides*)

# false agoseris, sagebrush false dandelion





**HABITAT** Shrub-steppe, grasslands, dry forests, lowland to high montane

**BLOOMS** Spring

**DESCRIPTION** Herbaceous perennial with milky juice, taprooted, stems 1 to few, erect, leafless, inflorescence a solitary head at the stem tip, plants 2–12 in. tall

**FLOWERS** Bracts of the head lance-shaped, about equal in length, hairy or not, tips long-pointed, all ray flowers, rays strap-shaped, yellow, ray tips finely toothed

**LEAVES** Basal only, wiry, blades linear to lance-shaped, 3–6 in. long, often with a white stripe down the center, surfaces hairy or not, edges wavy or smooth, tips pointed

**FRUIT** Achene, with a tuft of hair at the top

False agoseris is also known as sagebrush false dandelion, as it is often found in sagebrush communities and the flower has some similarities to common dandelion (*Taraxacum officinale*). False agoseris achenes are dispersed by the wind; the achene's hair tuft is aerodynamically designed to hold it aloft.

Asteraceae—aster family
*Senecio integerrimus*

# western groundsel, tall western groundsel, mountain butterweed





**HABITAT** Forests, meadows, shrub-steppe, lowland to subalpine

**BLOOMS** Spring, summer

**DESCRIPTION** Herbaceous perennial, hairs stiff or cobwebby, roots fibrous, stem 1, erect, flowers clustered in heads, stalked and several at the stem tip, the central head often larger, plants 8–24 in. tall

**FLOWERS** Bracts of the head in a single row, lance-shaped, usually black-tipped, both ray and disk flowers present, rays yellow, cream, or absent, disk flowers yellow or creamy white

**LEAVES** Basal and alternate on the stem, 2–9 in. long, stalked, blades oval, lance-, or heart-shaped, edges smooth or toothed, tips pointed, upper stem leaves shorter, stalkless

**FRUIT** Achene, with tuft of hair at the top

Western groundsel is native to the western United States and Canada, extending east to the Midwest. It has two varieties in our area: var. *ochroleucus* with yellowish white rays, and var. *exaltatus* (pictured) that has either bright yellow rays or is rayless with discoid heads.

Asteraceae—aster family

*Wyethia amplexicaulis*

# northern mule's ears, smooth dwarf sunflower

**HABITAT** Vernal wetlands, shrub-steppe, forests, meadows, lowland to mid-montane

**BLOOMS** Spring, summer

**DESCRIPTION** Herbaceous perennial, nonhairy, glandular, taprooted, stems erect to leaning, leaves stiff, shiny, inflorescence of several stalked, sunflower-like heads near the stem tip, plants 1–2½ ft. tall

**FLOWERS** Outer bracts of the head leaflike, inner bracts shorter, both ray and disk flowers present, rays bright to golden yellow, oval, 1–2 in. long, tips few-toothed, disk flowers yellow

**LEAVES** Basal and alternate along the stem, glandular, stalks short or absent, blades oval to lance-shaped, 8–24 in. long, edges smooth or toothed, tips pointed

**FRUIT** Achene, nonhairy

Northern mule's ears grows in vernally wet areas in shrub-steppe and dry forests. It can be confused with arrowleaf balsamroot (*Balsamorhiza sagittata*), which has solitary heads and soft, fuzzy grayish green leaves. White-headed wyethia (*W. helianthoides*) has white rays and grows in wetter habitats than northern mule's ears.

Boraginaceae—borage family
*Amsinckia lycopsoides*

## tarweed fiddleneck, bugloss fiddleneck

**HABITAT** Open forests, shrub-steppe, roadsides, disturbed areas, lowland to montane

**BLOOMS** Spring, summer

**DESCRIPTION** Annual, hairy, taprooted, stem erect, branched or not, inflorescence a curled cluster at the branch tips, unfurling as it blooms with flowers opening from the bottom up, plants 4–12 in. tall

**FLOWERS** Trumpet-shaped, yellow to orange with reddish orange spots at the base, sepals 5, similar in length, tips pointed, petal tube stiff-hairy within, 5-lobed, stamens 5, attached on the lower half of the petal tube

**LEAVES** Alternate along the stem and basal, blades oblong to lance-shaped, grayish green to green, with stiff and soft hairs, edges smooth, tips pointed, to 4 in. long

**FRUIT** Nutlet, surface bumpy

*Amsinckia* spp. are called fiddlenecks as the stem and coiled flower cluster resemble the neck and scroll of a fiddle. Tarweed fiddleneck is considered a weedy native as it thrives in disturbed areas. Fiddlenecks are toxic to livestock, damaging liver function.

Boraginaceae—borage family
*Lithospermum ruderale*

## Columbia puccoon, western gromwell, western stoneseed



**HABITAT** Shrub-steppe, dry forests, lowland to mid-montane

**BLOOMS** Spring

**DESCRIPTION** Herbaceous perennial, hairy, with a woody taproot, stems many, erect, unbranched, leafy, inflorescence of small, dense clusters of stalked flowers in the leaf axils, plants 8–24 in. tall

**FLOWERS** Trumpet-shaped, sepals 5, linear, long-hairy, petals pale greenish yellow, tube to ¼ in. long, glandular-hairy inside, 5-lobed, tips pointed, stamens 5

**LEAVES** Alternate, stalkless, blades linear to lance-shaped, 1–4 in. long, hairy, edges smooth, tips pointed, basal leaves absent

**FRUIT** Nutlet, grayish brown, smooth

The botanical name *Lithospermum* comes from the Greek words for stone and seed (*lithos* and *sperma*), referring to the hard nutlet fruit. Columbia puccoon grows among grasses in dry, open ponderosa pine (*Pinus ponderosa*) forests and in shrub-steppe communities with deeper soils. It grows well in dryland gardens in well-drained soils and sunny to partly shady locations.

Brassicaceae—mustard family
*Erysimum capitatum*

## western wallflower, rough wallflower





**HABITAT** Shrub-steppe, sand dunes, meadows, forest openings, lowland to alpine

**BLOOMS** Spring, summer

**DESCRIPTION** Biennial or short-lived herbaceous perennial, hairy, taprooted, stem 1, erect, inflorescence a dense, rounded flower cluster at the stem tip, plants 8–36 in. tall

**FLOWERS** Cross-shaped, stalked, sepals 4, oblong, green, petals 4, lemon-yellow to deep orange, sometimes reddish-tinged, round to egg-shaped, tips rounded, stamens 6, style 1

**LEAVES** Basal and alternate along the stem, blades linear, lance-, or spoon-shaped, 1–4½ in. long, T-shaped hairy, edges toothed or smooth, tips pointed

**FRUIT** Pod, linear, erect to curved upward

Western wallflower has unusual hairs on its foliage, branched at the midpoint into 2 or more segments. Most are T-shaped, but upper leaves can have hairs split into 3. Western wallflower attracts butterflies, making it a showy and butterfly-friendly addition to a dryland garden.

Cleomaceae—cleome family
*Peritoma lutea (Cleome lutea)*

## yellow bee plant



**HABITAT** Shrub-steppe, sandy flats, disturbed areas, lowland to middle elevations

**BLOOMS** Spring, summer

**DESCRIPTION** Annual, malodorous, nonhairy to sparsely hairy, taprooted, stem 1, branched or not, leafy, flowers in dense clusters at the branch tips, elongating in fruit, plants 1–3 ft. tall

**FLOWERS** Brushlike, sepals 4-lobed, yellowish, petals 4, bright yellow, oblong, stamens 6, protruding from the petals, pistil 1

**LEAVES** Alternate along the stem, stalked, blades divided into 5 leaflets, lance- to spoon-shaped, 1–2 in. long, edges smooth, tips pointed

**FRUIT** Pod, linear, nodding, seeds 10–20

Yellow bee plant thrives in disturbed areas within shrub-steppe communities, often on sandy or medium-textured soils. Its flowers bloom from late spring through summer, providing nectar for bees and butterflies when little else is in flower. Distinguish from similar species golden bee plant (*P. platycarpa*) and Rocky Mountain bee plant (*P. serrulata*) which have 3 leaflets instead of 5.

Crassulaceae—stonecrop family
*Sedum lanceolatum*

## lanceleaf stonecrop, spearleaf stonecrop





**HABITAT** Rocky areas, shrub-steppe, dry forests, lowland to alpine

**BLOOMS** Spring, summer

**DESCRIPTION** Succulent perennial, nonhairy, rhizomatous, stems erect, leafy, basal leaves in rosettes, flower clusters branched and flat-topped at the stem tips, plants 2–8 in. tall

**FLOWERS** Star-shaped, sepals 5, lance-triangular, tips pointed, petals 5, light to bright yellow, lance-shaped, tips pointed, stamens 10, pistil 1

**LEAVES** Basal and alternate along the stem, fleshy, linear to lance-shaped, green to reddish, to ¾ in. long, not curved, surfaces bumpy or not, edges smooth

**FRUIT** Pod, erect, 5 per flower, seeds many

Lanceleaf stonecrop can be distinguished from most other native sedums by its erect rather than spreading pods. One exception is curvedleaf stonecrop (*S. rupicola*), endemic to the Wenatchee Mountains of Washington, which is similar to lanceleaf stonecrop except for its curved, oval to egg-shaped stem leaves that detach easily from the stem. The detached leaves can root and form new individual plants.

Ericaceae—heath family
*Pterospora andromedea*

## pinedrops, woodland pinedrops

**HABITAT** Forests, woodlands, lowland to mid-montane

**BLOOMS** Summer

**DESCRIPTION** Herbaceous nonphotosynthetic perennial, roots nodular, forming a ball-like mass, stems 1 to several, unbranched, reddish brown, glandular-hairy, inflorescence an elongated cluster of nodding, stalked flowers at the stem tip, plants 1–3 ft. tall

**FLOWERS** Urn-shaped, to ¼ in. long, sepals 5, lance-shaped, reddish, glandular-hairy, petals 5-lobed, light yellow to cream, stamens 10, pistil 1

**LEAVES** Alternate, bractlike, lance-shaped to linear, crowded at the stem base

**FRUIT** Capsule, reddish brown, glandular-hairy, seeds many

Pinedrops is a mycotrophic species, parasitizing mycorrhizal fungi that are connected to tree roots. It grows in shady forests and woodlands. The name *Pterospora* is from the Greek words *pteron* (wing) and *sporos* (seed), referring to the morphology of its seeds. The netlike wing of the seed facilitates dispersal by air currents. Pinedrops stems are fleshy but harden as they dry, often persisting into the next year. The stems work well in dried plant arrangements.

Fabaceae—pea family
*Lupinus sulphureus*

# sulphur lupine





**HABITAT** Shrub-steppe, grasslands, lowland to mid-montane

**BLOOMS** Spring, summer

**DESCRIPTION** Herbaceous perennial, hairy, taprooted, stems numerous, erect, unbranched, leafy, basal leaves persistent, inflorescence spire-shaped with pealike flowers, plants 1–3 ft. tall

**FLOWERS** Pealike, sepals 2-lobed, silky-hairy, upper lobe with 2 teeth, petals 2-lipped, yellow, creamy white, blue, or violet, stamens 10, pistil 1

**LEAVES** Basal and alternate along the stem, stalked, blades palmately divided into 9–11 lance-shaped leaflets, surfaces hairy, edges smooth, tips pointed

**FRUIT** Pod, silky-hairy, 4–5 seeded

A key characteristic of sulphur lupine is its pealike flower with the 2 lips close together rather than spreading. It has two varieties: Bingen's lupine (var. *bingenensis*) with blue to violet flowers, and yellow lupine (var. *sulphureus*) with creamy white to yellow flowers. Kincaid's lupine (*L. oreganus* var. *kincaidii*) has similar flowers but has nonhairy pods. Kincaid's lupine grows west of the Cascade crest in Oregon and is rare in Washington.

Liliaceae—lily family
*Erythronium grandiflorum*

## glacier lily, yellow fawn-lily

**HABITAT** Meadows, slopes, forest openings, lowland to subalpine

**BLOOMS** Spring, summer

**DESCRIPTION** Herbaceous perennial from a slender bulb, ephemeral, nonhairy, stems erect, leafless, inflorescence of 1 to several stalked flowers at the stem tip, plants 6–12 in. tall

**FLOWERS** Star-shaped, nodding, tepals 6, pale to golden yellow, lance-shaped, 1–1¼ in. long, curling outward, tips pointed, stamens 6, anthers white, yellow, or red

**LEAVES** Basal only, blades lance-shaped, shiny green, edges smooth, tips pointed, 4–8 in. long

**FRUIT** Capsule, oblong, seeds many

Glacier lily is among the first species to bloom during the growing season, as its emergence is tied to snow-melt and soil temperature. Black and grizzly bears often dig up and consume the bulbs. While the bear activity decreases plant abundance, in the longer term, glacier lily populations increase due to higher soil nitrogen levels that spur plant growth and seed production.

Liliaceae—lily family
*Fritillaria pudica*

## yellow bells, yellow fritillary

**HABITAT** Shrub-steppe, open slopes, dry forests, rocky areas, lowland to mid-montane

**BLOOMS** Spring

**DESCRIPTION** Herbaceous perennial, ephemeral, nonhairy, the main bulb scaly with many rice-sized bulblets, stem 1, erect, leaves 2 or more, flower solitary at the stem tip, rarely 2–3, plants 4–12 in. tall

**FLOWERS** Bell-shaped, nodding, tepals 6, yellow to orangish yellow, oblong to lance-shaped, ½–1 in. long, edges smooth, tips rounded, stamens 6

**LEAVES** Lower pair mostly opposite, upper leaves if present may be alternate, blades linear to lance-shaped, 1–6 in. long, edges smooth, tips pointed

**FRUIT** Capsule, oblong, seeds many

A sign of spring's arrival, yellow bells bloom early, attracting bees and other insect pollinators to its floral rewards when little else is in flower. The yellow flowers fade to reddish brown after pollination, and as the capsule develops the stem straightens so that the fruit is held upright. Yellow bells is drought-tolerant and grows best in well-drained soils that are moist in spring but dry by summer.

Liliaceae—lily family
*Streptopus amplexifolius*

# clasping twisted-stalk

**HABITAT** Streambanks, forests, shrub thickets, lowland to subalpine

**BLOOMS** Spring, summer

**DESCRIPTION** Herbaceous perennial, rhizomatous, stems erect, branched, leafy, flowers solitary, rarely 2, nodding on bent stalks from the leaf axils, flowers beneath the leaves, plants 1½–4 ft. tall

**FLOWERS** Bell-shaped, tepals lance-shaped, greenish white to yellowish green, tips pointed and curved outward, stamens 6, pistil 1

**LEAVES** Alternate, blades lance- to egg-shaped, 2–4½ in. long, glossy green, clasping the stem, veins parallel, edges smooth or minutely toothed, tips pointed

**FRUIT** Berry, yellow to red, many-seeded

Clasping twisted-stalk may be confused with Hooker's fairy-bells (*Prosartes hookeri*), which has 1–3 bell-shaped flowers at the tips of the branches rather than in the leaf axils. Two other species of twisted-stalk occur in our area: rosy twisted-stalk (*S. lanceolatus*), which has tepals that are rose or white with reddish purple streaks, and small twisted-stalk (*S. streptopoides*), which has shorter, unbranched stems and greenish tepals with a purplish tinge.

Loasaceae—blazing-star family
*Mentzelia laevicaulis*

## giant blazing-star, smoothstem blazing-star

**HABITAT** Rocky slopes, shrub-steppe, dry forests, streambanks, roadsides, lowland to mid-montane

**BLOOMS** Summer

**DESCRIPTION** Biennial or a short-lived perennial, barbed-hairy, taprooted, stem 1, erect, whitish, branched, showy flowers in flat-topped clusters at the stem end and upper leaf axils, plants 1–3 ft. tall

**FLOWERS** Star-shaped, sepal lobes 5, linear, petals 5, lemon-yellow, lance-shaped, 1–3 in. long, tips pointed, stamens many, outer 5 stamens linear and petal-like, style 1

**LEAVES** Alternate along the stem and in basal rosettes, grayish green, to 6 in. long, blades linear, lance- to egg-shaped, surfaces barbed-hairy, edges lobed, tips pointed

**FRUIT** Capsule, oblong, ½–1 in. long, seeds many

Giant blazing-star grows in rocky, sandy, or gravelly soils in arid, sunny locales. Its leaves stick to animal fur and clothing due to having numerous barbed hairs. A good choice for use in native rock gardens, giant blazing-star is short-lived, but reseeds readily.

Orobanchaceae—broomrape family
*Castilleja thompsonii*

# Thompson's paintbrush

**HABITAT** Shrub-steppe, ridges, lowland to alpine

**BLOOMS** Spring, summer

**DESCRIPTION** Herbaceous perennial, long-hairy, taprooted, stems several, erect, green to reddish, inflorescence a brushlike cluster at the stem tip, plants 4–15 in. tall

**FLOWERS** Bracts showy, greenish yellow, cream, or reddish green, hairy, side lobes linear, paired, tips pointed, sepals tubular, reddish, 2-lobed, lobes notched, petals greenish, 2-lipped, upper lip slightly hooded, lower lip nonhairy, stamens 4

**LEAVES** Alternate, hairy, lower stem leaves linear, unlobed, upper stem leaves with paired linear side lobes, tips pointed

**FRUIT** Capsule, seeds many

Thompson's paintbrush, like other *Castilleja* spp., draws nutrients from its host, in this case sagebrush (*Artemisia* spp.), while also photosynthesizing and producing its own sugars, a condition called hemiparasitism. There are several other yellowish paintbrush species that grow in similar habitats as Thompson's paintbrush, such as Wallowa paintbrush (*C. oresbia*), which differs as it is short-hairy throughout, with a hairy, rather than nonhairy, lower petal lip.

Orobanchaceae—broomrape family
*Pedicularis bracteosa*

# bracted lousewort, towering lousewort, wood betony



**HABITAT** Forests, meadows, open slopes, mid-montane to alpine

**BLOOMS** Spring, summer

**DESCRIPTION** Herbaceous perennial, roots tuberous, fibrous, stems 1 to several, erect, unbranched, leaves fernlike, inflorescence a dense, spirelike cluster at the stem tip, plants 8–36 in. tall

**FLOWERS** Hoodlike, sepals hairy, tubular, 5-lobed, lobes linear, top lobe shorter than the rest, petals 2-lipped, ½–¾ in. long, yellow, reddish, purplish-tinged, or dark red to purple, upper lip hoodlike, lower lip 3-lobed

**LEAVES** Basal and alternate along the stem, blades lance-shaped, 3–10 in. long, pinnately divided into linear to lance-shaped lobes, lobe edges toothed to doubly toothed, tips pointed, basal leaves sometimes absent

**FRUIT** Capsule, curved, nonhairy

Bracted lousewort and other *Pedicularis* species are considered hemiparasites as they obtain nutrients through a combination of photosynthesis and parasitism. Hemiparasites have specialized rootlike structures called haustoria that penetrate the host plant's root system, forming a bridge between the two species.

Phrymaceae—lopseed family
*Erythranthe guttata (Mimulus guttatus)*

# yellow monkeyflower, seep-spring monkeyflower





**HABITAT** Seeps, streambanks, meadows, headlands, rock crevices, roadsides, lowland to mid-montane

**BLOOMS** Spring, summer

**DESCRIPTION** Herbaceous perennial, rhizomatous, stems square, erect, hairy, inflorescence of paired, stalked flowers from the upper leaf axils forming a loose cluster, plants 6–24 in. tall

**FLOWERS** Two-lipped, sepals green, tubular with 5 teeth, the top tooth longer than the rest, petals tubular, 2-lipped, yellow with maroon spots, upper lip 2-lobed, the lower lip larger, 3-lobed, ¼–¾ in. long, stamens 4

**LEAVES** Opposite, stalked or not, blades roundish, oval, or egg-shaped, to 5 in. long, 1 to 2 times longer than wide, edges variously toothed to lobed, tips rounded

**FRUIT** Capsule, seeds many

There are several other monkeyflower species with yellow flowers in our area. Plants with the following combination of traits are likely to be yellow monkeyflower: a perennial habit, maroon spots on the lower lip, top sepal tooth longer than the rest, a roundish leaf shape, and nonglandular hairs.

Plantaginaceae—plantain family
*Penstemon confertus*

# yellow penstemon, lesser yellow beardtongue

**HABITAT** Forest openings, meadows, riparian areas, lower to high montane

**BLOOMS** Spring, summer

**DESCRIPTION** Herbaceous perennial, rhizomatous, stems several, erect to curved at the base, non-hairy or short-hairy, flowers in dense, tiered clusters at the stem tip, plants 8–18 in. tall

**FLOWERS** Two-lipped, sepals 5-lobed, oblong to lance-shaped, edges raggedly toothed, tip long-pointed, petal tube narrow, upper lip 2-lobed, lower lip 3-lobed and hairy inside, pale yellow to yellowish white, stamens 5, 1 sterile

**LEAVES** Opposite along the stem, stalkless, blades lance- to egg-shaped, 1–4 in. long, edges smooth, tips pointed, basal leaves often absent, if present, are stalked and lance- to spoon-shaped

**FRUIT** Capsule, seeds many

Yellow penstemon is a delicately beautiful, relatively inconspicuous member of the *Penstemon* genus with its small, pale flowers. It is pollinated by bees including bumblebees, sweat bees, digger bees, and mining bees. Yellow penstemon grows well in garden settings, especially in rock or meadow gardens.

Polygonaceae—buckwheat family
*Eriogonum compositum*

## arrowleaf buckwheat, northern buckwheat, heartleaf buckwheat





**HABITAT** Talus slopes, rocky areas, shrub-steppe, woodlands, lowland to high montane

**BLOOMS** Spring, summer

**DESCRIPTION** Subshrub or herbaceous perennial, taprooted, stems erect to trailing, clump-forming, leaves basal only, inflorescence at the stem tip, in open, flat-topped clusters with bell-shaped bracts below, plants 1–2 ft. tall

**FLOWERS** Cup-shaped, tepals 6, pale to lemon-yellow, or creamy white, oblong to egg-shaped, nonhairy, tips rounded, flowers many per bell-shaped bract, stamens 9

**LEAVES** Basal only, stalked, blades lance- to heart-shaped, 3–10 in. long, upper surface hairy and greenish, the lower surface white woolly-hairy, edges smooth, tips pointed

**FRUIT** Achene, 3-angled, hairy

The two-toned leaves of arrowleaf buckwheat, green on top and whitish underneath, are helpful in identification. It thrives in arid habitats and varies in leaf shape and flower color. Arrowleaf buckwheat attracts butterflies and grows well in garden settings, preferring rocky soils and full sun to partial shade.

Polygonaceae—buckwheat family
*Eriogonum sphaerocephalum*





# rock buckwheat, round-headed desert buckwheat

**HABITAT** Shrub-steppe, dry forests, rocky or sandy flats and slopes, lowland to high montane

**BLOOMS** Spring, summer

**DESCRIPTION** Subshrub with a compact, rounded habit, taprooted, stems erect, much-branched, inflorescence with leafy, branched, ball-shaped clusters with bell-shaped bracts below, plants 2–15½ in. tall

**FLOWERS** Cup-shaped, tepals 6, yellow, white, yellowish white or pinkish, wedge- to egg-shaped, hairy, tips rounded, many-flowered per bell-shaped bract, stamens 9

**LEAVES** Basal and whorled below the inflorescence, blades linear, spatula-, or lance-shaped, ½–1 in. long, densely hairy below, nonhairy to hairy above but rarely densely so, edges rolled under or not, tips rounded or pointed

**FRUIT** Achene, top half hairy

Rock buckwheat varies in flower color, leaf characters, and inflorescence structure. It usually has several stalked flower clusters per branch end, but var. *sublineare*, scabland wild buckwheat, often has just one cluster per branch tip. Rock buckwheat has a pleasing, rounded habit and works well in dryland rock or pollinator gardens.

Polygonaceae—buckwheat family
*Eriogonum umbellatum*

## sulphur buckwheat, sulphur flower

**HABITAT** Rocky areas, shrub-steppe, forest openings, lowland to alpine

**BLOOMS** Summer

**DESCRIPTION** Subshrub or herbaceous, taprooted, stems many, trailing to erect, hairy, leafless or whorled at mid-length, flower clusters ball-shaped, branched or not, with leafy bracts beneath, plants 4–12 in. tall

**FLOWERS** Cup-shaped, tepals 6, nonhairy, spoon- to egg-shaped, width equal, pale to bright yellow, or cream, often pinkish-tinged, mostly either male or female

**LEAVES** Basal and sometimes whorled at stem mid-length, stalked, blades oblong, oval, spoon-, or egg-shaped, ¼–1 in. long, the lower surface grayish green, densely woolly-hairy, upper surface green, hairy, edges smooth, tips rounded or pointed

**FRUIT** Achene, nonhairy

Sulphur buckwheat is highly variable in leaf shape, inflorescence structure, and overall habit. It attracts bees and butterflies, growing well in rock gardens or on dry slopes. It thrives in full sun and well-drained sandy soils. The *Eriogonum* genus has about 250 species and is endemic to North America.

Ranunculaceae—buttercup family
*Ranunculus glaberrimus*

# sagebrush buttercup, smooth buttercup





**HABITAT** Shrub-steppe, dry forests, rocky areas, lowland to high montane

**BLOOMS** Spring

**DESCRIPTION** Herbaceous perennial, toxic when eaten, roots divided near the root crown, stems 1 or more, flowers 1 to several at the stem tips and upper leaf axils, plants 2–6 in. tall

**FLOWERS** Bowl-shaped, sepals 5, purplish-tinged, petals 5, glossy, bright yellow, egg-shaped, tips rounded, stamens and pistils many

**LEAVES** Basal and alternate along the stem, fleshy, blades oval to egg-shaped, ¼–2 in. long, nonhairy, edges smooth or lobed, tips mostly rounded

**FRUIT** Achene, egg-shaped with a hooklike tip, many per flower, each 1-seeded

Sagebrush buttercup has two varieties: var. *glaberrimus*, with lobed, egg-shaped basal leaves growing at lower elevations, and var. *ellipticus* with unlobed, oval basal leaves found at higher elevations. The glossy petals of sagebrush buttercup are due to their cell structure, which reflects light outward at different angles. This may serve to attract pollinators or to raise the temperature of the floral parts.

Rosaceae—rose family
*Drymocallis glandulosa*
(*Potentilla glandulosa*)

# sticky cinquefoil



**HABITAT** Meadows, roadsides, streambanks, forest openings, lowland to subalpine

**BLOOMS** Spring, summer

**DESCRIPTION** Herbaceous perennial, glandular-hairy, stems erect, reddish, flower clusters branched, open, at stem tips and in upper leaf axils, plants 6–36 in. tall

**FLOWERS** Disk-shaped, stalked, sepals 5 with smaller bracts in between, petals 5, creamy white to yellow, egg-shaped to roundish, slightly shorter than or equal to the sepals, stamens and pistils many, style spindle-shaped

**LEAVES** Basal and alternate along the stem, blades pinnately divided into 5–9 leaflets, oblong to egg-shaped, edges doubly toothed, sparsely to densely hairy

**FRUIT** Achene, reddish brown

Sticky cinquefoil was previously part of the *Potentilla* genus; it was reclassified based on DNA analysis and the morphology of the anther and style. *Drymocallis* spp. have styles that attach to the bottom half of the ovary and have anthers with one pollen chamber, while *Potentilla* spp. have styles attached near the top of the ovary and anthers with 2 pollen chambers.

Rosaceae—rose family
*Potentilla gracilis*

## fivefinger cinquefoil, slender cinquefoil, graceful cinquefoil

**HABITAT** Forests, meadows, shrub-steppe, lowland to subalpine

**BLOOMS** Summer

**DESCRIPTION** Herbaceous perennial, taprooted, stems several, hairy, branched, basal leaves many, stem leaves 1–2, inflorescence an open, branched, flat-topped cluster with few to many flowers, plants 1–2½ ft. tall

**FLOWERS** Bowl-shaped, sepals 5, lance-shaped, hairy, sometimes glandular, with bracts between the sepals, petals 5, bright yellow, heart-shaped, tips notched, stamens 20, pistils many

**LEAVES** Basal and alternate along the stem, stalked, blades palmately divided, leaflets 7–9, wedge- to lance-shaped, 1–3 in. long, woolly-hairy beneath, edges toothed to lobed, stem leaves smaller

**FRUIT** Achene, greenish

Fivefinger cinquefoil has several recognized varieties. It tolerates saline soils and does not form clonal patches. The invasive nonnative sulphur cinquefoil (*P. recta*) can be confused with fivefinger cinquefoil. Tell the two apart as sulphur cinquefoil has more than 2 stem leaves, few basal leaves that are not woolly-hairy beneath, and is patch-forming.

Rosaceae—rose family
*Purshia tridentata*

# bitterbrush, antelope-brush





**HABITAT** Shrub-steppe, dry forest openings, open slopes, lowland to mid-montane

**BLOOMS** Spring

**DESCRIPTION** Shrub, taprooted, stems much-branched, erect to spreading, twigs hairy, reddish brown to brown, flowers solitary on leafy, short spur shoots, plants 3–8 ft. tall

**FLOWERS** Funnel-shaped, sepals tubular, glandular-hairy, 5-lobed, lobes oblong to egg-shaped, to ¼ in. long, tips pointed, petals 5, yellow, yellowish white, or rarely white, spoon- to egg-shaped, tips rounded, stamens many, pistil 1

**LEAVES** Alternate, blades wedge-shaped, 3-lobed, ½–1 in. long, lower surface densely grayish-hairy, the upper surface greenish, tips rounded

**FRUIT** Achene, spindle-shaped, densely hairy, glandular

Bitterbrush is a long-lived, drought-resistant species, drawing water from a deep taproot. Its leaves are bitter-tasting, and the fruit (also bitter) contains a small amount of burgundy-colored liquid that Native Americans traditionally used to make a purple dye. Ungulates like elk and deer browse on bitterbrush foliage and rodents consume and cache the fruit, aiding seed dispersal.

Violaceae—violet family
*Viola glabella*

## stream violet, pioneer violet, smooth yellow violet

**HABITAT** Streambanks, forests, lowland to subalpine

**BLOOMS** Spring, summer

**DESCRIPTION** Herbaceous perennial, rhizomatous, stems 1 to several, arching to erect, only the upper stem leafy, flowers single, stalked from the leaf axils, plants 2–15 in. tall

**FLOWERS** Spurred, petals 5, to ½ in. long, both surfaces lemon-yellow, spur short, lower 3 petals purple-lined, stamens 5, style hairy at tip

**LEAVES** Basal and alternate along the stem, stalked, blades heart-shaped, 2–3½ in. long and about as wide, surfaces hairy or not, edges toothed, teeth tips rounded, leaf tips pointed

**FRUIT** Capsule, nonhairy, seeds dark brown

Violets are among the earliest plants to flower during the growing season. Distinguish steam violet from two other yellow-flowered species, evergreen violet (*V. sempervirens*) and round-leaved violet (*V. orbiculata*), both with mostly basal foliage and only 2–4 in. tall. Stream violet is taller and has stem leaves.

Violaceae—violet family
*Viola purpurea*

## goosefoot violet, purple-marked yellow violet





**HABITAT** Rocky slopes, forest openings, ridges, mid-montane to alpine

**BLOOMS** Spring, summer

**DESCRIPTION** Herbaceous perennial, purplish, hairy, rhizomatous, stems 1 to several, leafy, flowers solitary on longish stalks from the leaf axils, plants 1–10 in. tall

**FLOWERS** Spurred, spur short, petals 5, deep lemon-yellow, back of upper 2 petals maroon, the lower 3 petals brown-lined, the lateral 2 hairy near the base, stamens 5, style hairy at the tip

**LEAVES** Basal and alternate on the stem, blades diamond- to egg-shaped, ¼–2 in. long. Leaves are mostly longer than wide, but can be slightly shorter, which they seem to be in this photo. Veins prominent, the lower surface often purplish, edges usually toothed, tips rounded or pointed

**FRUIT** Capsule, spherical, short-hairy, seeds brown

Goosefoot violets are ssp. *venosa* in our area except in southern Oregon which are the taller ssp. *purpurea*. Distinguish goosefoot violet from the yellow-flowered Nuttall's violet (*V. nuttallii*) by the latter's larger oval to lance-shaped leaves with less-prominent veins and wavy edges. Nuttall's violet grows from low to high elevations.

# Orange Flowers

Malvaceae—mallow family
*Sphaeralcea munroana*

# Munro's globemallow, white-stemmed globemallow





**HABITAT** Shrub-steppe, grassy slopes, disturbed areas, lowland to mid-montane

**BLOOMS** Spring, summer

**DESCRIPTION** Herbaceous perennial, taprooted, stems several, upright, basal leaves absent, flowers in narrow, crowded clusters at the stem tips and from leaf axils, plants 8–30 in. tall

**FLOWERS** Bowl-shaped, stalked, sepals 5-lobed, star-shaped hairy, tips pointed, petals 5, apricot to reddish orange, egg-shaped, tips notched, to ½ in. long, stamens many, joined into a tube at the base, styles 12

**LEAVES** Alternate, stalked, blades triangular to egg-shaped, ½–2 in. long, shallowly 3–5-lobed or unlobed, edges toothed, surfaces star-shaped hairy, green or grayish green

**FRUIT** Capsule with 12 ear-shaped segments, star-shaped hairy, seeds 1 per segment

Gooseberry-leaved globemallow (*S. grossulariifolia*) might be mistaken for Munro's globemallow, but can be distinguished by its deeply lobed leaves and 2-seeded capsule segments. Munro's globemallow is drought-tolerant, grows easily from seed, prefers sandy to clay soils, and attracts a variety of bee and wasp pollinators.

Polemoniaceae—phlox family

*Collomia grandiflora*

# large-flowered collomia, large-flower mountain-trumpet

**HABITAT** Forest openings, edges, rocky slopes, meadows, lowland to mid-montane

**BLOOMS** Spring, summer

**DESCRIPTION** Annual, hairy to glandular-hairy, taprooted, stem 1, erect, branched or not, leafy, flowers in compact, round-topped clusters at the stem tip and from the leaf axils, plants 4–36 in. tall

**FLOWERS** Trumpet-shaped, stalkless, sepals 5-lobed, green, lobes triangular, tips pointed, petals 5-lobed, lobes oval, tips rounded, salmon-colored or yellowish white, ¾–1 in. long, stamens 5, attached to the inside of the petal tube, pollen blue to purple

**LEAVES** Alternate, stalkless, shiny green, linear to lance-shaped, 1–3 in. long, edges smooth, tips pointed

**FRUIT** Capsule, seeds 3

The showy trumpet-shaped flowers of large-flowered collomia are concentrated on the sides of the rounded clusters, while at the top are smaller cleistogamous, or closed, flowers. Cleistogamous flowers do not open, instead they are self-pollinated. The combination of open and closed flowers increases seed set while preserving the option of adaptation through genetic mixing between plants.

# Pink and Red Flowers

Amaryllidaceae—amaryllis family
*Allium acuminatum*

## taper-tip onion

**HABITAT** Rocky areas, meadows, shrub-steppe, forest openings, lowland to mid-montane

**BLOOMS** Spring, summer

**DESCRIPTION** Aromatic herbaceous perennial from an egg-shaped bulb, outer coat net-patterned, stem erect, nonhairy, leafless, flowers in a rounded cluster at the stem tip, plants 4–12 in. tall

**FLOWERS** Vase-shaped, stalked, tepals 6, light to purplish pink, sometimes white, lance-shaped, the outer 3 tepals wider and longer than the inner, tips pointed and curled back, stamens 6

**LEAVES** Basal, blades linear, round to somewhat flattened, tips pointed, 3–11½ in. long

**FRUIT** Capsule, seeds black

Taper-tip onion is edible with an oniony aroma and can be abundant in suitable habitats. Distinguish from similar species slim-leaf onion (*A. amplectens*) that has 6 similar-sized tepals with straight tips. Also similar looking is Blue Mountain onion (*A. dictuon*), rare and endemic to the Blue Mountains of Washington. Unlike taper-tip onion, Blue Mountain onion is rhizomatous, forming new bulbs each year and has straight rather than curled tepal tips.

Apocynaceae—dogbane family
*Apocynum androsaemifolium*

# spreading dogbane, mountain dogbane, bitter dogbane

**HABITAT** Forest openings, prairies, open slopes, meadows, lowland to subalpine

**BLOOMS** Summer

**DESCRIPTION** Toxic herbaceous perennial with milky-white sap, hairy or not, rhizomatous, stems erect, reddish, flower clusters at stem tips and sometimes from the leaf axils, plants 8–20 in. tall

**FLOWERS** Bell-shaped, pink to whitish, petal lobes 5, sepal lobes 5, both lance- to egg-shaped, stamens 5

**LEAVES** Opposite, stalked or not, drooping, blades oval to egg-shaped, 1–2¾ in. long, edges smooth, tips pointed, basal leaves absent

**FRUIT** Pod, 2–5½ in. long, erect or drooping, seeds with a tuft of hair at the top

A favorite nectar plant for butterflies and moths, spreading dogbane is found throughout most of North America. It is toxic to humans, livestock, and dogs, the latter the source of the name dogbane. Spreading dogbane can be distinguished from similar species hemp dogbane (*A. cannabinum*) as the latter has greenish white flowers and leaves held upright instead of drooping.

Apocynaceae—dogbane family
*Asclepias speciosa*

## showy milkweed

**HABITAT** Streambanks, roadsides, seasonal wetlands, lowland to mid-montane

**BLOOMS** Spring, summer

**DESCRIPTION** Herbaceous perennial with milky sap, rhizomatous, stems 1 to several, erect, hairy, mostly unbranched, leaves fleshy, inflorescence 1 to several flat-topped to rounded, stalked clusters from the leaf axils, plants 1–4 ft. tall

**FLOWERS** Star-shaped, sepals 5, greenish, hairy, petals 5, pinkish to purplish red, bent downward, with 5 pink to rose slipper-shaped nectar cups around the column of stamens

**LEAVES** Opposite, stalked, oblong to egg-shaped, green, hairy, 4–8 in. long, edges smooth, tips pointed

**FRUIT** Pod, egg-shaped, warty-spiny, about 4 in. long, seeds with hair tuft at top

Milkweed species are key plants for bees and butterflies, particularly for monarch butterflies (*Danaus plexippus*) as milkweeds are their only larval host. The milky sap of milkweed contains chemicals toxic to many animals, deterring herbivory, but others, like monarch caterpillars, are not affected. Showy milkweed grows well in garden settings and is a good choice for a pollinator garden.

Asteraceae—aster family
*Antennaria microphylla (Antennaria rosea)*

# rosy pussytoes, rosy everlasting, small-leaf pussytoes





**HABITAT** Balds, meadows, forest openings, rocky slopes, lowland to alpine

**BLOOMS** Spring, summer

**DESCRIPTION** Herbaceous mat-forming perennial, grayish-hairy, separate male- and female-flowered plants, stoloniferous, stems erect, inflorescence a flat-topped cluster at the stem tip, plants 4–12 in. tall

**FLOWERS** Bracts of the head in overlapping shingled rows, bracts pink to rose, white, or yellow, rays absent, disk flowers whitish

**LEAVES** Basal and alternate along the stem, grayish green, densely woolly-hairy, edges smooth, tips pointed, ¼–1½ in. long, basal leaves many, lance- to spatula-shaped, stem leaves linear

**FRUIT** Achene, smooth or with small, rounded bumps

In alpine habitats rosy pussytoes may be confused with alpine pussytoes (*A. alpina*), which has brownish green to black bracts of the floral head. Many pussytoe species produce seeds at least partially through apomixis, without fertilization of the ovule. Seeds produced through apomixis are genetically the same as the parent plant.

Asteraceae—aster family

*Erigeron poliospermus* var. *poliospermus*

## cushion fleabane, hairy-seeded daisy, purple cushion fleabane

**HABITAT** Shrub-steppe, rocky areas, dry forests, lowland to middle elevations

**BLOOMS** Spring

**DESCRIPTION** Herbaceous perennial, taprooted, stems many, erect, unbranched, spreading-hairy, glandular, flower head solitary at the stem tip, plants 2–6 in. tall

**FLOWERS** Bracts of the head in rows, lance-shaped, tips pointed, most with both ray and disk flowers, rays pink, purple, or violet, disk flowers yellow

**LEAVES** Basal and alternate along the stem, blades linear to lance-shaped, spreading-hairy, 1–3 in. long, edges smooth, tips pointed, upper stem leaves few and smaller

**FRUIT** Achene, densely long-hairy, with a hair tuft at the top

Kittitas fleabane (*E. poliospermus* var. *cereus*) has branched stems, multiple heads, and is endemic to central Washington. Distinguish cushion fleabane from similar species shaggy fleabane (*E. pumilus*) by looking at the achene. The achene surface is clearly visible in shaggy fleabane fruits, while those of cushion fleabane are hidden due to being densely hairy.

Brassicaceae—mustard family
*Phoenicaulis cheiranthoides*

# daggerpod

**HABITAT** Shrub-steppe, rocky areas, forest openings, lowland to high montane

**BLOOMS** Spring, summer

**DESCRIPTION** Herbaceous perennial, taprooted, stems 1 to many, reddish, trailing to erect, flowers stalked in a rounded cluster at the stem tip, plants 2–8 in. tall

**FLOWERS** Cross-shaped, sepals 4, oblong, petals 4, pinkish, lavender, or reddish purple, egg- to lance-shaped, to ½ in. long, tips rounded, stamens 6, pistil 1

**LEAVES** Basal and alternate along the stem, grayish green, basal leaves stalked, blades lance-shaped, 1–6 in. long, surfaces with branched hairs, stem leaves smaller, stalkless

**FRUIT** Pod, linear to lance-shaped, nonhairy, ¾–3 in. long, spreading, seeds many

Daggerpod is common in lithosol areas within shrub-steppe, dry forests, and at higher elevations on rocky slopes and outcrops. When the pods are mature, the entire flowering stem separates from the plant in one piece and tumbles with the wind, dispersing the seeds along the way. Daggerpod is the only species in its genus.

Cactaceae—cactus family
*Pediocactus nigrispinus*
(*Pediocactus simpsonii*)

## basalt cactus, snowball cactus





**HABITAT** Shrub-steppe, rock outcrops, lowland to mid-montane

**BLOOMS** Spring, summer

**DESCRIPTION** Fleshy perennial, taproot short, divided into many fibrous roots, stems 1 to many, oblong to globe-shaped, green, spiny, flowers in a dense cluster on stem tip, plants 2–12 in. tall

**FLOWERS** Showy, tepals many, outer tepals reddish brown, oblong to wedge-shaped, inner tepals pale to deep pink, white, or yellowish, oval to lance-shaped, stamens many

**LEAVES** Modified into spines, central spines linear, straight, reddish brown to black, to 1 in. long, marginal spines shorter, white to yellowish brown

**FRUIT** Dry, globe-shaped, reddish brown, seeds many

Basalt cactus is a rare species, endemic to Washington, Oregon, and Idaho. Growing low to the ground, basalt cactus blends into its often rocky surroundings unless in flower. The blooms open only on sunny days, remaining closed when cloudy. Vulnerable to collecting pressure, basalt cactus grows slowly and does not survive transplantation. It is best enjoyed in its natural habitat.

Ericaceae—heath family
*Arctostaphylos uva-ursi*

## kinnikinnick, bearberry

**HABITAT** Rocky or sandy areas, coastal bluffs, prairies, open forests, lowland to alpine

**BLOOMS** Spring, summer

**DESCRIPTION** Shrub, mat-forming, stems trailing, sometimes rooting at the nodes, bark reddish brown, hairy, sometimes glandular, leaves evergreen, inflorescence a dense, few-flowered cluster at the branch tips, plants 2–6 in. tall

**FLOWERS** Urn-shaped, pink to whitish, petal lobes 5, pink, sepal tube short, lobes 5, tips rounded, flowers stalked

**LEAVES** Alternate, evergreen, stalked, blades spoon- to egg-shaped, ½–1 in. long, dark green, sparsely hairy, tips rounded

**FRUIT** Berry, bright red, edible but insipid

Mats of kinnikinnick can be several feet across and it grows nicely as a groundcover in the garden. Pinemat manzanita (*A. nevadensis*) is similar in appearance to kinnikinnick but has pointed leaf tips, white flowers, brownish red berries, and grows at mid-montane elevations and above.

Ericaceae—heath family
*Chimaphila umbellata*

## pipsissewa, western prince's-pine

| | |
|---|---|
| **HABITAT** | Conifer forests, lowland to mid-montane |
| **BLOOMS** | Summer |
| **DESCRIPTION** | Evergreen subshrub, rhizomatous, stems erect, green or reddish, often branched, inflorescence a cluster of 3–10 nodding, stalked flowers at the stem tip, plants 4–12 in. tall |
| **FLOWERS** | Saucer-shaped, nodding on short stalks, sepals 5, less than ⅛ in. long, petals egg-shaped, pinkish to rose, to ⅜ in. long, stamens 10, pistil 1 |
| **LEAVES** | Whorled, evergreen, stalked, blades lance-shaped, 1¼–3 in. long, shiny green, nonhairy, edges smooth or toothed, tips pointed |
| **FRUIT** | Capsule, round, with many tiny seeds |

Pipsissewa is a circumboreal species found in shady forests. Distinguish it from the closely related little prince's-pine (*C. menziesii*), which is smaller with wider, oval leaves, and usually has 1–3 flowers. Pipsissewa contains a number of bioactive phytochemicals that researchers are studying for their potential in treating disease.

Fabaceae—pea family
*Lathyrus nevadensis*

## Sierra pea, purple peavine

**HABITAT** Forests, meadows, grassy slopes, lowland to subalpine

**BLOOMS** Spring, summer

**DESCRIPTION** Herbaceous perennial, rhizomatous, stems climbing or erect, clusters of 2–10 stalked flowers from the leaf axils, plants 6–30 in. tall

**FLOWERS** Pealike, 2-lipped, ½–1 in. long, bluish or reddish purple, pinkish, or rarely white, upper lip often darker than the lower lip, sepals hairy, 5-lobed, stamens 10, style hairy on one side

**LEAVES** Alternate, stalked, blades pinnately divided into oval to egg-shaped leaflets, ¾–2½ in. long, tendril present, sometimes reduced to a bristle

**FRUIT** Pod, nonhairy, 1–2¾ in. long

Wild peas (*Lathyrus* spp.) can sometimes be confused with the vetches (*Vicia* spp.) as both groups are viny with similar-shaped flowers and leaves. To distinguish wild peas from vetches, look closely at the style. The style of wild peas are hairy on one side, like a toothbrush, while vetch styles are hairy all around, like a bottlebrush.

Fabaceae—pea family
*Trifolium macrocephalum*

# big-head clover, giant-head clover





**HABITAT** Shrub-steppe, forest openings, lowland to mid-montane

**BLOOMS** Spring

**DESCRIPTION** Herbaceous perennial, hairy, rhizomatous, stems erect to trailing, leafy, inflorescence a round to oblong, densely flowered cluster at the stem tip, plants 4–12 in. tall

**FLOWERS** Two-lipped, sepals tubular, 5-toothed, teeth needlelike, much longer than the tube, feathery-hairy, petals often 2-colored, white with pink to rose, stamens 10

**LEAVES** Basal and alternate along the stem, stalked, blades palmately divided into 5–9 leaflets, lance- to heart-shaped, surfaces hairy below and hairy or not above, edges sharp-toothed, tips pointed, rounded, or notched

**FRUIT** Pod, 1-seeded

Big-head clover has showy, often 2-toned flowers gathered into a headlike cluster. It grows in rocky, clay, or deep well-drained soils in arid areas. Big-head clover is common in lithosol shrub-steppe, rocky grasslands, openings in ponderosa pine (*Pinus ponderosa*), and Garry oak (*Quercus garryana*) forests or in juniper (*Juniperus* spp.) woodlands.

Geraniaceae—geranium family
*Geranium viscosissimum*

## sticky geranium



**HABITAT** Forest openings, meadows, slopes, lowland to mid-montane

**BLOOMS** Spring, summer

**DESCRIPTION** Herbaceous perennial, taprooted, stems 1 to several, erect to curved at the base, branched, mostly glandular-hairy, flower clusters open and branched near the stem tip, plants 1–3 ft. tall

**FLOWERS** Saucer-shaped, showy, stalked, sepals 5, glandular-hairy, petals 5, roundish, rose-pink to lavender, rarely whitish, inner surface hairy, stamens 10

**LEAVES** Basal and opposite on the stem, often glandular, stalked, blades 2–4½ in. wide, deeply 5–7-lobed, lobes wedge-shaped, edges irregularly toothed, tips pointed

**FRUIT** Capsule, glandular-hairy, long-beaked at the top

Sticky geranium occurs east of the Cascade crest in Washington and Oregon. In western Oregon the similar Oregon crane's-bill (*G. oreganum*) may be seen, especially in oak woodlands and prairies. Besides the geographical differences, petals of Oregon crane's-bill are not hairy on the inner surface. Oregon crane's-bill is thought to be extirpated from Washington.

Iridaceae—iris family
*Olsynium douglasii*

## grass-widow, purple-eyed grass-widow, satinflower

**HABITAT** Rocky areas, woodlands, vernal wetlands, lowland to mid-montane

**BLOOMS** Winter, spring

**DESCRIPTION** Herbaceous perennial, roots fibrous, stems 1 to several, unbranched, leaves grasslike, inflorescence of 1–3 nodding, stalked flowers at the stem tip, plants 4–12 in. tall

**FLOWERS** Bell-shaped, to ¾ in. long, tepals 6, lance- to egg-shaped, light to dark reddish purple, satiny, tips rounded or pointed, stamens 3, joined at the base, pistil 1, stigmas 3-lobed

**LEAVES** Grasslike, alternate on the stem, linear, dark green, 2–6 in. long, tips pointed, basal leaves reduced, bractlike

**FRUIT** Capsule, egg-shaped, seeds brown

Blooming early in the growing season, grass-widow often grows in seasonal wetlands that dry up by summer. Ephemeral, the aboveground parts wither after the fruit matures. Grass-widow has two varieties: var. *inflatum* has an inflated, globe-shaped stamen tube, and var. *douglasii* has a nonglobe-shaped stamen tube. It makes an attractive addition to rock gardens.

Liliaceae—lily family
*Calochortus macrocarpus*

## sagebrush mariposa lily, green-banded mariposa lily

**HABITAT** Shrub-steppe, grassy slopes, open forests, lowland to middle elevations

**BLOOMS** Spring, summer

**DESCRIPTION** Herbaceous perennial, roots fibrous, stem erect, unbranched, leaves grasslike, tulip-like flowers 1–3 at the stem tip, plants 8–18 in. tall

**FLOWERS** Bell-shaped, sepals 3, lance-shaped, greenish, petals 3, egg-shaped with a pointed tip, pinkish, lavender, or white, outer surface with a green stripe, nectar gland with yellow hairs near inner petal base, stamens 6

**LEAVES** Alternate along the stem and basal, linear, tips pointed and curled, basal leaves wither early

**FRUIT** Capsule, linear to lance-shaped, seeds many

Sagebrush mariposa lily is widely distributed but often overlooked due to its grasslike appearance when not in flower and its later flowering period. May be confused with long-bearded sego lily (*C. longebarbatus*), rare in Washington and Oregon, which has white hairs near the nectar gland, rounded petal tips, and grows in vernally moist meadows and edge habitat.

Malvaceae—mallow family
*Sidalcea oregana*

## Oregon checker-mallow, marsh hollyhock





**HABITAT** Meadows, streambanks, forest openings, shrub-steppe, lower to mid-montane

**BLOOMS** Spring, summer

**DESCRIPTION** Herbaceous perennial, hairs simple to star-shaped, taprooted, stems 1 to several, erect to curved at the base, inflorescence spirelike or open, plants 8–60 in. tall

**FLOWERS** Bowl-shaped, light to deep pink, stalked, sepals 5-lobed, petals 5, egg-shaped, tips notched, to ¾ in. long, stamens many, joined at the base, styles several, bisexual or female only

**LEAVES** Basal and alternate along the stem, stalked, blades heart-shaped to rounded, 1–4 in. long and wide, surfaces hairy or nonhairy, edges mostly 5–9-lobed, tips pointed

**FRUIT** Capsule with ear-shaped segments, segments 1-seeded

Oregon checker-mallow has three recognized varieties, separated largely by the type and degree of hairiness and geographic range. One variety, Wenatchee checker-mallow (var. *calva*), is listed as endangered by Washington State and the federal Endangered Species Act. Cultivars of Oregon checker-mallow are available through the nursery trade.

Melanthiaceae—bunchflower family
*Trillium petiolatum*

# roundleaf trillium, purple trillium





**HABITAT** Streambanks, meadows, forests, lowland to mid-montane

**BLOOMS** Spring

**DESCRIPTION** Herbaceous perennial, ephemeral, nonhairy, rhizomatous, stem 1, erect, flower solitary, surrounded by 3 large leaves, plants 2–7 in. tall

**FLOWERS** Egg-shaped, sepals 3, green, oblong to oval, petals 3, maroon, reddish brown, or yellowish, linear to lance-shaped, 1–2 in. long, often curved upward, stamens 6, stigmas 3

**LEAVES** Whorled in a group of 3, stalked, blades round to egg-shaped, 3–5 in. long and almost as wide, dark green, edges smooth, tips rounded

**FRUIT** Berrylike capsule, egg-shaped, seeds many

Roundleaf trillium is endemic to eastern Washington, Oregon, and Idaho. It has a fleshy, berrylike capsule that is shed whole from the plant. *Trillium* seeds have an oily, fleshy structure called an elaiosome that functions to aid seed dispersal as it is attractive to ants. Deer also disperse seed by eating the fruit with the seeds passing through undigested.

Montiaceae—spring beauty family
*Claytonia lanceolata*

## western springbeauty, lanceleaf springbeauty





**HABITAT** Grassy slopes, meadows, forests, shrub-steppe, lowland to alpine

**BLOOMS** Spring, summer

**DESCRIPTION** Herbaceous perennial from a bulblike corm, nonhairy, stems 1 to several, basal leaves present but withering early, flowers in an open, often 1-sided cluster, plants 2–8 in. tall

**FLOWERS** Saucer-shaped, stalked, sepals 2, petals 5, white to pink, often pinkish-lined, sometimes yellow, oblong to lance-shaped, ¼–½ in. long, tips notched, stamens 5, styles 3

**LEAVES** Basal leaves stalked, lance-shaped, stem leaves opposite, stalkless, lance- to egg-shaped, 1–3 in. long, edges smooth, tips pointed

**FRUIT** Capsule, egg-shaped, seeds shiny black with elaiosome

Western springbeauty seeds have elaiosomes, fleshy bits that attract ants. The ants aid seed dispersal as they carry the seeds back to their colony. Similar species broad-leaved springbeauty (*C. cordifolia*) is rhizomatous and has heart-shaped leaves. The rare Pacific lance-leaved springbeauty (*C. multiscapa* ssp. *pacifica*), found in Washington's Olympic Mountains, has stalked stem leaves and unnotched petals.

Montiaceae—spring beauty family
*Lewisia rediviva*

# bitterroot, resurrection flower

**HABITAT** Rocky areas, shrub-steppe, forest openings, lowland to mid-montane

**BLOOMS** Spring, summer

**DESCRIPTION** Herbaceous perennial, ephemeral, taprooted, flowering stems with a whorl of bracts at mid-length, leaves fleshy, flowers solitary, showy, plants ½–1 in. tall

**FLOWERS** Bowl-shaped, sepals 6–9, oval to egg-shaped, ¼–1 in. long, unequal, rose, pink, or whitish, tips rounded, petals 10–19, lance-shaped, ½–1¼ in. long, light to deep pinkish rose, sometimes whitish, stamens 30–50, anthers pink

**LEAVES** Basal only, fleshy, blades linear, dark green, mostly withering before the buds open

**FRUIT** Capsule, seeds dark brown

One of our most striking native flowers, bitterroot leaves emerge early, radiating from a central point, looking rather like the tentacles of a sea anemone. As the buds form, the leaves wither and are often gone before the flowers open, so that the flower dazzles on its own. The taproot is harvested by native peoples for use as a foodstuff.

Onagraceae—evening primrose family
*Chamaenerion angustifolium (Chamerion angustifolium, Epilobium angustifolium)*

## fireweed

**HABITAT** Open slopes, roadsides, disturbed areas, meadows, lowland to subalpine

**BLOOMS** Spring, summer

**DESCRIPTION** Herbaceous perennial, rhizomatous, patch-forming, stems erect, rarely branched, leafy, inflorescence a spirelike cluster at the stem tip, plants 3–10 ft. tall

**FLOWERS** Trumpet-shaped, deep rose pink to purple, sepals and petals 4, petals egg-shaped, ¼–¾ in. long, sepals lance-shaped, stamens 8, stigmas 4-lobed

**LEAVES** Alternate, blades lance-shaped, 2–8 in. long, green with a white central vein, edges smooth, tips pointed

**FRUIT** Capsule, podlike, to 3 in. long, seeds many, with a tuft of silky hair at the top

Fireweed seeds are light and easily carried by the wind, dispersing far from the parent plant. The seeds readily germinate in areas that have burned or are otherwise disturbed. Fireweed rapidly forms large patches in such places, creating a sea of rosy pink flowers, admired by humans and visited by hummingbirds and bees in search of nectar.

Onagraceae—evening primrose family
*Clarkia pulchella*

## ragged robin, Elkhorn clarkia, pink fairies



**HABITAT** Forest openings, roadsides, slopes, lowland to mid-montane

**BLOOMS** Spring, summer

**DESCRIPTION** Annual, finely hairy, taprooted, stems erect, branched, inflorescence an open cluster of several stalked flowers at the branch tips, plants 4–19½ in. tall

**FLOWERS** Plate-shaped, showy, sepals 4, curved together on one side after the bud opens, petals 4, rose pink to purple, 3-lobed, lobe tips rounded, with 2 small teeth near petal base, stamens 8, 4 fertile, stigma 4-lobed

**LEAVES** Alternate, blades linear to lance-shaped, 1–3 in. long, edges smooth or toothed, tips pointed

**FRUIT** Capsule, hairy, to ¾ in. long, seeds dark brown

Ragged robin is also known as deer horn as the lobed petals are reminiscent of deer antlers. It is easy to grow in the garden from seed; for best results, sow in fall in a sunny area using sandy to rocky soil. Ragged robin colonizes disturbed areas and is often abundant on recently burned sites.

Onagraceae—evening primrose family
*Epilobium ciliatum*

## common willowherb, Watson's willowherb, ciliate willowherb

**HABITAT** Lakeshores, streambanks, roadsides, meadows, forest openings, lowland to mid-montane

**BLOOMS** Summer

**DESCRIPTION** Herbaceous perennial, hairy, taprooted, stems erect, branched, with open, branched flower clusters at the stem and branch tips, plants 1–2 ft. tall

**FLOWERS** Funnel-shaped, sepals 4, lance-shaped, petals 4, egg-shaped, white, pink, or rose, to ½ in. long, tips notched, stamens 8, stigma not lobed

**LEAVES** Opposite, basal leaf rosettes often present, 1–4½ in. long, blades lance- to egg-shaped, usually hairy, edges toothed

**FRUIT** Capsule, linear, ½–3 in. long, glandular-hairy, seeds many, with a hair tuft at the top

Common willowherb occurs throughout most of North America, in southern South America, and temperate parts of Asia. Its seeds are dispersed by wind, the hair tuft acting as a parachute carrying seeds away from the parent plant. The name willowherb comes from the similarity of its leaf shape, long and slender, to that of many willows (*Salix* spp.).

Orchidaceae—orchid family
*Corallorhiza maculata*

# spotted coralroot, summer coralroot

**HABITAT** Forests, often in deep shade, lowland to mid-montane

**BLOOMS** Spring, summer

**DESCRIPTION** Herbaceous perennial, parasitic, rhizomatous, stems purplish to reddish brown, rarely yellow, inflorescence a narrow, open cluster of short-stalked flowers at the stem tip, plants 8–16 in. tall

**FLOWERS** Hoodlike, sepals 3, lance-shaped, reddish brown, purplish, or rarely yellow, curved, 3-nerved, to ¼ in. long, petals 3, 2 similar to the sepals, the 3rd liplike, oval to egg-shaped, white with wine-red spots, to ¼ in. long, edges lobed, tip rounded, stamens and pistil fused into a curved column

**LEAVES** Reduced to alternate membranous bracts

**FRUIT** Capsule, nodding, egg-shaped, seeds numerous

The name coralroot refers to the knobby, coral-like appearance of the genus's rhizomes. Spotted coralroot is parasitic on soil fungi, forming mycorrhizal associations and transferring nutrients from the fungal mycelium to the orchid. Ozette coralroot, var. *ozettensis*, lacks spots on the lip and is endemic to the northwestern part of Washington's Olympic Peninsula.

Orobanchaceae—broomrape family
*Castilleja hispida*

## harsh paintbrush

**HABITAT** Prairies, forest openings, lowland to mid-montane

**BLOOMS** Spring, summer

**DESCRIPTION** Herbaceous perennial, hairy, taprooted, stems several, erect, inflorescence a brushlike cluster at the stem tip, plants 8–24 in. tall

**FLOWERS** Bracts showy, red, orange, or yellow, hairy, lobed, lobes linear, tips rounded, sepals tubular, 2-lobed, lobes notched, petals greenish, tubular, 2-lipped, upper lip hooded, stamens 4

**LEAVES** Alternate, blades lance-shaped, hairy, lower leaves unlobed, upper stem leaves with 1–2 pairs of narrow side lobes, tips rounded, lower leaves smaller than upper stem leaves

**FRUIT** Capsule, seeds cone-shaped, tan

Harsh paintbrush hybridizes with other paintbrushes (*Castilleja* spp.) where their populations overlap. Although paintbrushes are green and photosynthesize, they also obtain nutrients from nearby plants, often grasses, a condition called hemiparasitism. Hemiparasites can survive without a host plant but are healthier with one. Harsh paintbrush is a known larval host for the rare Taylor's checkerspot butterfly.

Orobanchaceae—broomrape family
*Castilleja miniata*

# giant red paintbrush, scarlet paintbrush, slender paintbrush

**HABITAT** Prairies, meadows, forests, lowland to subalpine

**BLOOMS** Spring, summer

**DESCRIPTION** Herbaceous perennial, taprooted, stems erect, often branched, inflorescence a brushlike cluster at the stem tip, plants 8–30 in. tall

**FLOWERS** Bracts showy, oval to egg-shaped, bright red to scarlet, rarely purplish or yellow, hairy, tips toothed or not, sepals tubular, 2-lobed, lobes toothed, tips pointed, petals greenish, 2-lipped, upper lip hooded, stamens 4

**LEAVES** Alternate, blades linear to lance-shaped, hairy or not, edges mostly smooth, tips pointed

**FRUIT** Capsule, seeds many, tiny

Giant red paintbrush has a wide ecological amplitude and is broadly distributed across the Pacific Northwest. Distinguish it from harsh paintbrush (*C. hispida*) by its larger size, fewer hairs, and the lack of lobing on leaves and bracts. Along the coast it may be confused with coast paintbrush (*C. litoralis*) that has leaning stems, wider egg-shaped leaves with rounded tips, and floral bracts with side lobes and a rounded central tip.

Orobanchaceae—broomrape family
*Pedicularis groenlandica*

## elephant's head lousewort





**HABITAT** Wet meadows, seeps, streambanks, mid-montane to subalpine

**BLOOMS** Summer

**DESCRIPTION** Herbaceous perennial, nonhairy, roots fibrous, stems 1 to several, erect, unbranched, reddish, leaves fernlike, inflorescence a dense, spirelike cluster at the stem tip, plants 6–24 in. tall

**FLOWERS** Hoodlike, sepals tubular, 5-lobed, petals 2-lipped, pink, pinkish purple, or red, the hoodlike upper lip resembling an elephant's head, longer than the lower lip

**LEAVES** Basal and alternate on the stem, stalked, blades lance-shaped, 2–10 in. long, edges lobed and toothed, tips pointed

**FRUIT** Capsule, curved, nonhairy

Similar species little elephant's head (*P. attollens*) grows in the Oregon Cascades, the Steens Mountain area, and south into the Sierra Mountains of California. Distinguish elephant's head lousewort from little elephant's head by the relative lengths of the upper and lower petal lips. Little elephant's head has a longer lower lip compared to the upper, while in elephant's head lousewort the upper lip is longer than the lower.

Orobanchaceae—broomrape family
*Pedicularis racemosa*

## sickletop lousewort, leafy lousewort

**HABITAT** Coniferous forests, dry meadows, rocky slopes, mid-montane to subalpine

**BLOOMS** Summer

**DESCRIPTION** Herbaceous perennial, nonhairy, roots fibrous, stems usually several, erect, unbranched, leafy, inflorescence an open, leafy cluster at the stem tip, with smaller, stalked clusters from the upper leaf axils, plants 6–18 in. tall

**FLOWERS** Hoodlike, sepals 2-lobed, petals 2-lipped, pinkish white, cream, or purple, tip of the hoodlike upper lip curled inward toward the lower lip, ½ in. long

**LEAVES** Alternate, blades lance-shaped, 1–3 in. long, edges toothed, tips pointed

**FRUIT** Capsule, curved, nonhairy

Sickletop lousewort and other *Pedicularis* species are exclusively pollinated by bumblebees, with studies showing that no seeds are produced when bumblebees are absent. Coiled-beak lousewort (*P. contorta*) flowers are similar to those of sickletop lousewort, but the plant has divided leaves and lacks leafy bracts with the flowers. The name lousewort originated from the superstition that the plant harbored lice and infected livestock that grazed nearby.

Paeoniaceae—peony family
*Paeonia brownii*

# Brown's peony, western peony

**HABITAT** Shrub-steppe, dry forests, meadows, low to high montane

**BLOOMS** Spring

**DESCRIPTION** Herbaceous perennial, nonhairy, roots fleshy, stems several, erect to leaning, flowers nodding, solitary at the stem tips, plants 8–24 in. tall

**FLOWERS** Bowl-shaped, sepals 5, oval, purplish green to green, petals 5, ¼–½ in. long, round, smaller than the sepals, reddish brown to purplish, edges yellow to greenish, stamens many, styles 5

**LEAVES** Alternate, leathery, bluish green, blades divided into 3 leaflets, edges lobed, tips pointed

**FRUIT** Pod, ¾–1½ in. long, seeds blackish purple, 2–5 seeded

Brown's peony grows throughout the West, one of two species in the *Paeonia* genus native to North America. Its flowers are pollinated by wasps, sweat bees, and flies. Seeds are dispersed by rodents that gather and store them in underground caches. Brown's peony can be grown from seed in dryland gardens, preferring deeper soils and sun to partial shade.

Polemoniaceae—phlox family
*Collomia linearis*

## narrow-leaf collomia, tiny trumpet





**HABITAT** Shrub-steppe, rocky areas, forest openings, lowland to mid-montane

**BLOOMS** Spring, summer

**DESCRIPTION** Annual, hairy to glandular-hairy, taprooted, stem 1, erect, flowers in compact, round-topped clusters at the stem tip and from upper leaf axils, plants 4–24 in. tall

**FLOWERS** Trumpet-shaped, stalkless, sepals 5-lobed, green, lobes triangular, petals tubular, pink, blue, or white, to ½ in. long, 5-lobed, lobes oblong, tips rounded, stamens 5, pollen white to blue

**LEAVES** Alternate, stalkless, green, linear to lance-shaped, ¼–2¾ in. long, edges smooth, tips pointed

**FRUIT** Capsule, seeds 3

Narrow-leaf collomia may be confused with yellow-staining collomia (*C. tinctoria*), which also has pink flowers and grows on rocky slopes. Distinguish them by yellow-staining collomia's small, 2–5 flowered clusters in the axils of the much-branched stem. Narrow-leaf collomia colonizes disturbed sites and is widespread. The genus name *Collomia* is derived from the word *kolla*, Greek for glue, a reference to the seeds that become sticky when moistened.

Polemoniaceae—phlox family
*Ipomopsis aggregata (Gilia aggregata)*

## scarlet gilia, skyrocket





**HABITAT** Open slopes, rocky areas, forest openings, roadsides, lowland to high montane

**BLOOMS** Spring, summer

**DESCRIPTION** Short-lived perennial, taprooted, stems 1 to several, erect, glandular-hairy, flowers in 1-sided, branched clusters along the upper stem, plants 8–36 in. tall

**FLOWERS** Trumpet-shaped, ½–1 in. long, petals tubular with 5 lobes, scarlet red or yellowish, with white to red speckles, lobes triangular, tips pointed, sepals 5, linear, stamens 5

**LEAVES** Basal and alternate along the stem, 1–3 in. long, blades divided into many linear leaflets, hairy or not, basal leaves wither before the flowers open

**FRUIT** Capsule, oblong, 3-chambered, few seeds per chamber

A scarlet gilia plant flowers once and then dies, although it may live for several years as a cluster of basal leaves before blooming. This type of plant is called a monocarpic perennial. Although short-lived, scarlet gilia reseeds readily. The scarlet red blooms are pollinated by hummingbirds, while yellowish flowers are pollinated by moths.

Polemoniaceae—phlox family
*Phlox longifolia*

# longleaf phlox

**HABITAT** Forests, shrub-steppe, open slopes, lowland to mid-montane

**BLOOMS** Spring

**DESCRIPTION** Subshrub or herbaceous, glandular-hairy, hairy, or nonhairy, taprooted, stems many, branched, leafy, flowers fragrant in flat-topped clusters at the stem tips, plants 4–16 in. tall

**FLOWERS** Trumpet-shaped, fragrant, sepals 5-lobed, lobes linear, petal tube 5-lobed, pink to white, lobes egg-shaped, tips rounded, sepals shorter than the petal tube, stamens 5, style to ½ in. long, much longer than the stigmas

**LEAVES** Opposite, blades linear, ½–3 in. long, edges smooth, tips pointed, stalk absent

**FRUIT** Capsule, oval, seeds few

Longleaf phlox can have a compact, rounded habit or be somewhat leggy. Similar species showy phlox (*P. speciosa*) can be distinguished by its notched petal lobes and its style that is shorter than the stigmas. Distinguish sticky phlox (*P. viscida*) from longleaf phlox by its malodorous scent and copiously glandular-hairy sepals that are greater than or equal to the petal tube length.

Polemoniaceae—phlox family
*Phlox speciosa*

## showy phlox





**HABITAT** Shrub-steppe, dry forest openings, meadows, lowland to mid-montane

**BLOOMS** Spring

**DESCRIPTION** Subshrub, glandular-hairy, taprooted, stems many, erect, branched, leafy, flowers stalked, in flat-topped leafy clusters near the stem and branch tips, plants 4–16 in. tall

**FLOWERS** Trumpet-shaped, sepals 5-lobed, linear, glandular-hairy, tips pointed, petals tubular, 5-lobed, pink to white, lobes heart-shaped, tips notched, sepals nearly as long as the petal tube, stamens 5, style to 1⁄16 in. long, mostly shorter than the stigmas

**LEAVES** Opposite, blades linear to lance-shaped, ½–3 in. long, surfaces glandular-hairy or just hairy, edges smooth, tips pointed, stalk absent

**FRUIT** Capsule, oval, seeds few

Showy phlox and other phlox species have trumpet-shaped flowers with a long floral tube and petal lobes that spread horizontally, held at a 90-degree angle. The lobes' flat surface makes an ideal landing spot for butterflies, one of the main pollinators of phlox. They are also pollinated by moths and long-tongued bees.

Polygonaceae—buckwheat family
*Eriogonum thymoides*

## thyme buckwheat, thyme-leaved buckwheat





**HABITAT** Shrub-steppe, forest openings, rocky areas, lowland to middle elevations

**BLOOMS** Spring

**DESCRIPTION** Shrub with a compact, rounded habit, densely hairy, taprooted, stems many-branched, inflorescence a ball-shaped cluster at the stem tips, plants 2–6 in. tall

**FLOWERS** Cup-shaped, tepals 6-lobed, rosy red, yellow, white, or a mix of colors, lobes wedge- to egg-shaped, densely hairy, tips rounded, flowers mostly either male or female

**LEAVES** Basal with 1 whorl on the flower stem, blades linear to spatula-shaped, to ¼ in. long, green to grayish green, hairy, edges rolled under, tips rounded

**FRUIT** Achene, hairy only near the top

Thyme buckwheat usually grows on sites with thin soils such as in lithosol shrub-steppe, rock outcrops, or along ridgetops. A lovely miniature shrub, thyme buckwheat is a delight that can add interest to a garden throughout the growing season. In spring red buds open into yellowish or white flowers, while in fall the leaves turn reddish pink.

Primulaceae—primrose family

*Dodecatheon conjugens* (*Primula conjugens*)

## Bonneville shooting star, desert shooting star

**HABITAT** Vernally wet areas, seeps, in shrub-steppe and dry forests, lower to middle elevations

**BLOOMS** Spring

**DESCRIPTION** Herbaceous perennial, glandular-hairy or not, roots fibrous, stem 1, erect, flower clusters of 1 to several nodding flowers at the stem tips, plants 4–12 in. tall

**FLOWERS** Nodding, sepal lobes 5, bent back, lance-shaped, petal lobes 5, bent back, sword-shaped, pink to rose-pink, yellow at the base with a reddish purple band, stamens 5, mostly distinct, maroon or yellow, pistil 1

**LEAVES** Basal only, stalked, blades lance- to spoon-shaped, 1–5 in. long, hairy or not, edges smooth, tips pointed

**FRUIT** Capsule, oblong to egg-shaped, seeds many

Bonneville shooting star grows in vernally moist areas within arid habitats. Stamens of *Dodecatheon* flowers are designed to release pollen when "buzzed" by bumblebees. Buzz pollination occurs when a bee hangs from the stamens and vibrates its thoracic muscles, shaking pollen from the anthers onto the bee's abdomen.

Primulaceae—primrose family
*Dodecatheon pulchellum* (*Primula pauciflora*, *Dodecatheon cusickii*)

## few-flowered shooting star, Cusick's shooting star

**HABITAT** Vernally wet areas in shrub-steppe and dry forests, swamps, lowland to high montane

**BLOOMS** Spring, summer

**DESCRIPTION** Herbaceous perennial, glandular-hairy or not, roots fibrous, stem 1, erect, unbranched, leafless, inflorescence a compact cluster of stalked, nodding flowers at the stem tip, plants 4–17½ in. tall

**FLOWERS** Nodding, sepal lobes 5, petal lobes 5, ¼–¾ in. long, bent back, sword-shaped, lavender to purplish grading to yellow at the base, stamens joined, maroon or yellow

**LEAVES** Basal only, 2–10 in. long, blades lance- to spoon-shaped, tapering to the stalk, edges smooth or toothed, tips pointed

**FRUIT** Capsule, seeds many

Few-flowered shooting star is quite variable with several recognized varieties, one of which, alkali meadow shooting star (*D. pulchellum* var. *shoshonense*), is rare in Oregon. Unlike Bonneville shooting star (*D. conjugens*), which has separate stamens, the stamens of few-flowered shooting star are joined together.

Ranunculaceae—buttercup family
*Aquilegia formosa*

## red columbine, western columbine, Sitka columbine

**HABITAT** Forest openings, meadows, lowland to mid-montane

**BLOOMS** Spring, summer

**DESCRIPTION** Herbaceous perennial, hairy or not, often glandular, taprooted, stems several, erect, inflorescence 1 to several stalked, nodding flowers at the stem tip and from upper leaf axils, plants 6–36 in. tall

**FLOWERS** Spurred, sepals 5, petal-like, pale to dark red, up to 1 in. long, spurs straight, sepal lobes lance-shaped, spreading, tips pointed, petals 5, yellow, tips rounded, stamens many

**LEAVES** Basal and alternate along the stem, stalked, blades palmately divided into 3 leaflets, leaflets egg-shaped, lobed, tips rounded

**FRUIT** Pod, glandular-hairy, ½–1 in. long, seeds several

Red columbine grows well in garden settings, preferring rich soil and partial shade. It attracts bees, butterflies, and hummingbirds. Yellow columbine (*A. flavescens*) looks similar to red columbine but has yellow flowers with curved spurs and grows primarily on talus slopes and high-mountain meadows. The two species form hybrids where their populations overlap.

Rosaceae—rose family
*Geum triflorum*

## prairie smoke, old man's whiskers





**HABITAT** Dry forests, meadows, rocky areas, lowland to subalpine

**BLOOMS** Spring, summer

**DESCRIPTION** Herbaceous perennial, rhizomatous, stems 1 to several, hairy, erect, with one set of opposite leaves at mid-length, inflorescence a cluster of nodding flowers at the stem tip, plants 4–12 in. tall

**FLOWERS** Vase-shaped, sepals 5-lobed, lobes triangular with linear bracts between, reddish purple, pink, or yellowish, petals 5, yellowish, pink, or purplish-tinged, oval to egg-shaped, stamens and styles many

**LEAVES** Basal and opposite on the stem, hairy, stalked, blades 2–6 in. long, oblong to egg-shaped, divided into wedge-shaped leaflets, leaflet edges lobed, tips pointed

**FRUIT** Achene, topped by a purplish featherlike style

Prairie smoke has a quiet, subdued beauty when in flower and a showy brashness in fruit. The nodding bloom straightens as the fruit develops and the many featherlike styles lengthen to 1 in. long. The purplish, long feathery styles en masse resemble smoke puffs, the source of the name prairie smoke.

Saxifragaceae—saxifrage family

*Lithophragma glabrum* (*Lithophragma bulbifera*)

## bulbiferous prairie star, bulbiferous woodland star, smooth fringecup

**HABITAT** Shrub-steppe, dry forests, meadows, lowland to subalpine

**BLOOMS** Spring, summer

**DESCRIPTION** Herbaceous perennial, ephemeral, glandular-hairy, rhizomatous, with bulblets among the roots, stems erect, reddish purple, inflorescence a flat-topped cluster of 2–5 stalked flowers or solitary, some flowers replaced by bulblets, plants 2–10 in. tall

**FLOWERS** Starlike, sepals cup-shaped, 5-lobed, glandular-hairy, petals 5, pale to purplish pink, mostly 5-lobed, tips pointed, stamens 10

**LEAVES** Basal and alternate along the stem, stalked, blades divided into 3 leaflets, leaflets wedge-shaped, 3-lobed, may have bulblets in leaf axils

**FRUIT** Capsule, seeds brownish, with tiny spines

Bulbiferous prairie star forms vegetative propagules called bulblets. Each can grow into an individual plant that is genetically identical to the parent plant. Seeds produce plants with genetic differences, due to the process of sexual reproduction. Bulbiferous prairie star often grows alongside small-flowered prairie star (*L. parviflorum*), which lacks bulblets aboveground and has 3-lobed petals.

Saxifragaceae—saxifrage family
*Lithophragma parviflorum*

## small-flowered prairie star, small-flowered woodland star, small-flowered fringecup

**HABITAT** Prairies, coastal bluffs, balds, forest openings, lowland to mid-montane

**BLOOMS** Spring

**DESCRIPTION** Herbaceous perennial, ephemeral, glandular-hairy, rhizomatous, with bulblets among the roots, stem erect, purplish, inflorescence a cluster of 5–15 stalked, delicate flowers at the stem tip, plants 4–12 in. tall

**FLOWERS** Starlike, showy, sepal tube vase-shaped, 5-lobed, petals 5, pink to whitish, 3-lobed, stamens 10

**LEAVES** Basal and alternate along the stem, stalked, blades ½–1 in. across, divided into 3–5 leaflets, leaflets 3-lobed, stem leaves few, much smaller than the basal leaves

**FRUIT** Capsule, seeds many, brown, wrinkled

Similar species bulbiferous woodland star (*L. glabrum*) has petals that are 5-lobed, often has reddish bulblets in the leaf axils, and has minutely spiny seeds. Small-flowered prairie star blooms while soils are moist in spring and the aboveground plant parts wither after the fruit have matured. The plant lives on through its root system until spring arrives once more.

# Blue and Violet Flowers

Asparagaceae—asparagus family
*Camassia quamash*

## common camas, small camas

**HABITAT** Wet meadows, prairies, open slopes, lowland to mid-montane

**BLOOMS** Spring

**DESCRIPTION** Herbaceous perennial, nonhairy, ephemeral, with egg-shaped bulb, diameter ½–1 in., flowers stalked, clustered at the stem tip, tepals not twisting together, withering separately, plants 6–30 in. tall

**FLOWERS** Light blue to deep blue-violet, tepals 6, equally sized, ½–1¼ in. long, stamens 6, anthers yellow or violet, stigmas 3

**LEAVES** Basal only, grasslike, linear to lance-shaped, 4–24 in. long, edges smooth, tips pointed

**FRUIT** Capsule, oval to egg-shaped, seeds black, shiny

Common camas has several geographic varieties. It grows in similar habitats as great camas (*C. leichtlinii*), but has slightly irregular flowers, with 1 tepal curving downward while the rest curve upward, and the tepals remain separate as they wither. Native Americans consider bulbs of common camas to be a treasured edible. It can be propagated easily by seed and grows well in a garden setting.

Asparagaceae—asparagus family
*Triteleia grandiflora* var. *grandiflora*
(*Brodiaea douglasii*)

# large-flowered triteleia, Douglas' brodiaea

**HABITAT** Shrub-steppe, grasslands, forest openings, lowland to mid-montane

**BLOOMS** Spring, summer

**DESCRIPTION** Herbaceous perennial from a bulb, nonhairy, stem 1, erect, leaves grasslike, flower cluster umbrella-like at the stem tip, plants 8–28 in. tall

**FLOWERS** Bell-shaped, ½–1 in. long, pale to deep bluish purple or white, tepals 6-lobed, lobes oblong to lance-shaped, edges wavy, stamens 6, unequally attached inside the petal tube, pistil 1

**LEAVES** Basal only, 1–3, blades linear to lance-shaped, 10–20 in. long, tips pointed

**FRUIT** Capsule, egg-shaped, seeds many, black

Large-flowered triteleia has a grasslike appearance when not in flower. To propagate, collect mature black seeds and plant in well-drained soil outdoors. Seeds need to be in cool temperatures for a month or longer to germinate. As with other bulb-based species, it will take several years for the plants to bloom from a seedling, as the bulb develops slowly.

Asteraceae—aster family
*Erigeron filifolius*

## threadleaf fleabane, threadleaf daisy





**HABITAT** Shrub-steppe, grasslands, dry forests, rocky areas, lowland to mid-montane

**BLOOMS** Spring, summer

**DESCRIPTION** Herbaceous perennial, grayish green, taprooted, stems many, erect, stiff-hairy, leafy, flowers clustered in heads, heads in a flat-topped cluster or solitary at the stem tips, plants 4–19 in. tall

**FLOWERS** Bracts of the head in rows, similar in length, oval, hairy, glandular, or both, tips pointed, both ray and disk flowers present, rays blue, white, or pink, to ½ in. long, disk flowers yellow

**LEAVES** Alternate along the stem and basal, blades linear, stiff-hairy, ¼–3 in. long, edges smooth, tips pointed

**FRUIT** Achene, hairy, with tuft of hair at top

Threadleaf fleabane forms attractive clumps, their grayish green foliage topped by showy daisylike flowers. The hairs of the plant are appressed, meaning they lie flat along the surface. Threadleaf fleabane attracts bees and butterflies and can easily be grown in well-drained sandy or rocky garden beds.

Asteraceae—aster family
*Erigeron speciosus*

## showy fleabane, showy daisy

**HABITAT** Forest openings, edges, meadows, lowland to high montane

**BLOOMS** Summer, fall

**DESCRIPTION** Herbaceous perennial, rhizomatous, roots fibrous, stems clustered, erect, nonhairy to sparsely short-hairy, inflorescence a flat-topped cluster of heads near the stem tip, plants 6–30 in. tall

**FLOWERS** Bracts of the head in rows, linear to lance-shaped, glandular, tips pointed, both ray and disk flowers present, rays blue, lavender, or rarely white, to ½ in. long, disk flowers yellow

**LEAVES** Basal and alternate along the stem, basal leaves wither early, basal and lower stem leaves stalked, blades lance-shaped, 1–3 in. long, edges fringed with hair, tips pointed

**FRUIT** Achene, sparsely hairy, with hair tuft at the top

A summer bloomer, showy fleabane works well for meadow and pollinator gardens, attracting a wide variety of insects. Three-veined fleabane (*E. subtrinervis*) is similar to showy fleabane but is more densely hairy, grows in somewhat drier habitats, and has not been recorded in Oregon.

Boraginaceae—borage family
*Hackelia micrantha*

## blue stickseed, Jessica's stickseed, meadow forget-me-not

**HABITAT** Forest openings, meadows, streambanks, lower montane to subalpine

**BLOOMS** Spring, summer

**DESCRIPTION** Herbaceous perennial, hairy, taprooted, stems several, erect, inflorescence of compact flower clusters on longish stalks from the upper leaf axils, plants 1–3 ft. tall

**FLOWERS** Trumpet-shaped, sepals 5, petals 5-lobed, blue, sometimes whitish, with a whitish or yellow eye, lobes egg-shaped, stamens 5

**LEAVES** Basal and alternate along the stem, blades oval to lance-shaped, 2–13 in. long, stalked except for on the upper stem, hairy, edges smooth, tips pointed

**FRUIT** Nutlet, pear-shaped, prickles numerous

Blue stickseed is in the same family as forget-me-nots (*Myosotis* spp.) and has similar flowers. The name stickseed refers to the numerous prickles on the surface of the nutlet fruit. The fruit are dispersed by sticking to animal hair or clothing. To facilitate attachment, the flower stalks curve downward as the fruit matures, making contact between fruit and animal more likely.

Boraginaceae—borage family
*Mertensia longiflora*

# trumpet bluebells, trumpet lungwort, leafy bluebells





**HABITAT** Shrub-steppe, grassy slopes, forests, lowland to mid-montane

**BLOOMS** Spring

**DESCRIPTION** Herbaceous perennial, ephemeral, with shallow, tuberous roots, stems 1–2, erect, flowers nodding in a compact cluster at the stem tip, plants 2–10 in. tall

**FLOWERS** Bell-shaped, sepals 5-lobed, lance-shaped, petals tubular, 5-lobed, blue, purplish, or pink, tube 2–3 times longer than the lobes, stamens 5, pistil 1

**LEAVES** Alternate, stalkless, blades lance-shaped, hairy or not, ¾–2 in. long, edges smooth, tips rounded, basal leaves often absent

**FRUIT** Nutlet, surface wrinkled

Flowers of trumpet bluebells change color as they age, from purplish pink buds to deep blue once open, both stages often present at the same time. Leafy bluebells (*M. foliosa*) can be confused with trumpet bluebells; distinguish it by its many stems, the deep-seated, stout root system, evident basal leaves, and a floral tube less than twice as long as the lobes.

Boraginaceae—borage family
*Mertensia paniculata*

## tall bluebells, tall lungwort





**HABITAT** Streambanks, meadows, forest edges, mid-montane to subalpine

**BLOOMS** Spring, summer

**DESCRIPTION** Herbaceous perennial, rhizomatous or not, stems several, leafy, with branched, open clusters of nodding flowers on slender stalks from the upper leaf axils, plants 6–60 in. tall

**FLOWERS** Bell-shaped, nodding, blue to pink, ¼–½ in. long, sepals 5, linear, hairy, petals tubular, 5-lobed, tips pointed, stamens 5, pistil 1

**LEAVES** Basal and alternate along the stem, stalked, basal blades heart-shaped, stem leaf blades lance- to egg-shaped, edges smooth, tips pointed

**FRUIT** Nutlet, wrinkled

Tall bluebells ranges from Alaska across most of Canada and dips down into the United States in the Pacific Northwest and the upper Midwest. It is shade tolerant and pollinated by bees. Like all species in the borage family, tall bluebells has a type of fruit called a nutlet, a small hard structure usually containing 1 seed. Tall bluebells would make a good addition to a meadow garden, preferring well-drained, rich soils.

Fabaceae—pea family
*Astragalus purshii*

## woolly-pod milkvetch, Pursh's woolly-pod, woolly-pod locoweed

**HABITAT** Shrub-steppe, disturbed areas, open forest, lowland to subalpine

**BLOOMS** Spring, summer

**DESCRIPTION** Low herbaceous perennial, woolly-hairy, taprooted, stems several, prostrate, to 5 in. long, leaves pealike, inflorescence a compact cluster of less than 10 stalked flowers at the stem tip

**FLOWERS** Two-lipped, ½–1 in. long, pinkish purple, cream, white, or lavender-tinged, upper lip larger than the lower, sepal tube grayish-hairy, teeth 5, linear to lance-shaped, stamens 10

**LEAVES** Basal only, or also alternate on the stem, stalked, pinnately divided into 5–17 leaflets, leaflets egg- to lance-shaped, or roundish, surfaces woolly-hairy, tips rounded or pointed

**FRUIT** Pod, egg-shaped, curved, tip pointed, white woolly-hairy

Woolly-pod milkvetch primarily grows in sandy or thin, rocky soils, tolerates disturbance, and is found throughout the West. The pods collect around the base of the plant when shed, and often persist into the following year. The pod's densely white-hairy surface and curved shape aid identification when not in flower.

Fabaceae—pea family
*Lupinus lepidus* var. *aridus*

# dry-ground lupine, prairie lupine

**HABITAT** Shrub-steppe, meadows, dry forests, lowland to mid-montane

**BLOOMS** Spring

**DESCRIPTION** Herbaceous perennial, silky-hairy, taprooted, foliage grayish green, stems 1 to several, short, leafy, flowers in spire-shaped clusters, spire partially hidden by the leaves, plants 4–14 in. tavll

**FLOWERS** Pealike, stalked, sepals 2-lobed, hairy, upper lobe divided, petals 2-lipped, blue, violet, or pink, the upper lip marked with white

**LEAVES** Basal and alternate along the stem, long-stalked, blades palmately divided into 5–9 lance-shaped leaflets, surfaces equally long silky-hairy, edges smooth, tips pointed

**FRUIT** Pod, hairy, ¼–¾ in. long, seeds 2–4

Lupines are primarily pollinated by bees, and the genus has evolved in ways that benefit both plant and pollinator. Bees see blue and purple well, and interpret yellow as blue, and most native lupines are shades of these colors. Bees forage from the bottom of an inflorescence upward and lupine spires bloom from the bottom up, matching the bee's behavior.

Fabaceae—pea family
*Lupinus sericeus*

# silky lupine



**HABITAT** Dry forests, shrub-steppe, prairies, lowland to subalpine

**BLOOMS** Spring, summer

**DESCRIPTION** Herbaceous perennial, silky-hairy, taprooted, foliage silvery grayish green, stems 1 to several, branched or not, leafy, inflorescence spire-shaped with pealike flowers, plants 8–36 in. tall

**FLOWERS** Pealike, stalked, sepals 2-lobed, silky-hairy, upper lobe split in 2, petals 2-lipped, lavender, blue, or sometimes white, upper lip hairy on the back, marked inside with white, yellow, or brown (in white flowers), lower lip cup-shaped

**LEAVES** Alternate along the stem, stalked, blades palmately divided into 7–9 lance-shaped leaflets, surfaces equally silky-hairy, edges smooth, tips pointed, basal leaves mostly absent

**FRUIT** Pod, silky-hairy, seeds 3–5

Silky lupine grows throughout Canada and the western United States except for California. It grows in a variety of soil and habitat types and is most abundant in lower to mid-montane zones. Silky lupine, like all *Lupinus* spp., can thrive in low-nitrogen soils as they can change atmospheric nitrogen to a bioavailable form.

Hydrophyllaceae—waterleaf family
*Hydrophyllum capitatum* var. *capitatum*

## ballhead waterleaf

**HABITAT** Forests, meadows, lowland to mid-montane

**BLOOMS** Spring

**DESCRIPTION** Herbaceous perennial, hairy, roots fibrous with a very short rhizome, stems 1 to few, leaves taller than the flower clusters, clusters dense and round on short stalks, plants 4–16 in. tall

**FLOWERS** Funnel-shaped, sepals 5, linear to oblong, bristly-hairy, tips pointed, petal tube 5-lobed, lavender to purplish blue, sometimes white, lobes oblong, stamens 5, pistil 1, stamens and pistil protruding from the flower

**LEAVES** Basal and alternate on lower stem, long-stalked, blades pinnately divided into 7–11 leaflets, leaflets wedge-shaped, mostly 3-lobed

**FRUIT** Capsule, seeds 1–3

Ballhead waterleaf blooms early in the growing season, preferring vernally moist soils. There are two other recognized varieties of the species, var. *thompsonii*, grandma's pincushion, with flower clusters held above the leaves and found mostly in the Columbia Gorge, and var. *alpinum*, woolen breeches, with clusters close to ground level and found at high elevations in Oregon.

Hydrophyllaceae—waterleaf family
*Phacelia linearis*

## thread-leaf phacelia





**HABITAT** Shrub-steppe, sand dunes, rocky slopes, forests, lowland to mid-montane

**BLOOMS** Spring

**DESCRIPTION** Annual, hairy, taprooted, stem 1, erect, branched or not, flowers in small clusters from the upper leaf axils and stem tip, plants 4–20 in. tall

**FLOWERS** Funnel-shaped, to ½ in. long, sepals 5, linear, bristly-hairy, petals 5-lobed, lavender, violet, or deep blue, lobes egg-shaped, tips rounded, stamens 5, style 1 with a shallowly lobed tip

**LEAVES** Alternate, blades linear to lance-shaped, ¼–3 in. long, surfaces densely hairy, edges smooth or lobed, tips pointed

**FRUIT** Capsule, egg-shaped, hairy, seeds 6–15

The flowers of thread-leaf phacelia are showy and attract a variety of insects. It is widespread throughout eastern Washington and Oregon in suitable habitats. Less common is similar species low phacelia (*P. humilis*). Distinguish it from thread-leaf phacelia by its wider, oval to egg-shaped leaves and its smaller, ¼ in. long, deep blue to purple flowers with a deeply lobed style.

Iridaceae—iris family
*Iris missouriensis*

## Rocky Mountain iris, western blue iris, western blue flag

**HABITAT** Seeps, seasonal wetlands, lowland to mid-montane

**BLOOMS** Spring, summer

**DESCRIPTION** Herbaceous perennial, clump-forming, rhizomatous, flowering stems 1 to many, erect, unbranched, 2–4 flowers with stalks near the stem tip, leafy bracts below, plants 8–24 in. tall

**FLOWERS** Showy, pale to deep blue, or whitish, with purple lines, sepals 3, spreading, lance-shaped, edges wavy, tips rounded, with a central yellow stripe, petals erect, lance-shaped, shorter than the sepals, edges wavy

**LEAVES** Basal only, blades linear to sword-shaped, mostly erect, nonhairy, tips pointed

**FRUIT** Capsule, 2 in. long, seeds many, brown

Rocky Mountain iris thrives in seasonally wet areas within arid habitats such as sagebrush (*Artemisia* spp.) steppe and ponderosa pine (*Pinus ponderosa*) forests. It does not tolerate year-round wet soils. Rocky Mountain iris is pollinated mostly by bumblebees and hummingbirds. It grows well in garden settings that can simulate its natural habitat.

Lamiaceae—mint family

*Monardella odoratissima*

## mountain monardella, western mountain balm, coyote mint

**HABITAT** Rocky slopes, meadows, shrub-steppe, forest openings, mid-montane to subalpine

**BLOOMS** Spring, summer

**DESCRIPTION** Subshrub or herbaceous perennial, aromatic, taprooted, stems many, square, erect to curved, mostly unbranched, flower clusters dense, flat-topped with egg-shaped bracts beneath at the stem tips, plants 4–18 in. tall

**FLOWERS** Two-lipped, sepals 5-lobed, lobes triangular, hairy, petals lavender, pink, or white, upper lip 2-lobed, lower lip 3-lobed, tips pointed, stamens 4, pistil 1

**LEAVES** Opposite, grayish green or green, stalks short or absent, blades oval to lance-shaped, ½–1½ in. long, surfaces hairy, edges smooth, tips pointed

**FRUIT** Nutlet

Mountain monardella has a rounded habit and its dense, flat-topped flower clusters attract butterflies and bees. It makes a nice addition to rock and butterfly gardens. Plant it in sandy to rocky, well-drained soil in sunny locations. Mountain monardella is in the mint family, and its leaves, like those of other mints, are edible.

Lamiaceae—mint family
*Salvia dorrii*

## purple sage, Dorr's sage, gray ball sage

**HABITAT** Shrub-steppe, rocky slopes, lowland to middle elevations

**BLOOMS** Spring, summer

**DESCRIPTION** Aromatic shrub, glandular and hairy, taprooted, stems erect to spreading, much-branched, rigid, leaves silvery gray, flowers in dense, tiered clusters at the branch tips, plants 4–24 in. tall

**FLOWERS** Two-lipped, bluish violet, fragrant, sepals reddish purple, upper lip 2-lobed, lower lip larger, stamens 2, style 1, bracts below the flower clusters reddish purple

**LEAVES** Opposite, evergreen, blades oval to spoon-shaped, ½–1 in. long, grayish green, glandular and powdery-hairy, edges smooth, tips rounded or pointed

**FRUIT** Nutlet, smooth

Purple sage is an attractive woody shrub with a spicy odor. It requires little maintenance in dryland gardens as it is resistant to deer browse, is drought tolerant, and maintains its shape without pruning. The shape and color of purple sage flowers attracts bee visits. Bees often exhibit constancy, repeatedly visiting flowers of one species once identified as a good food source, aiding pollination.

Linaceae—flax family
*Linum lewisii* var. *lewisii*

## wild blue flax, Lewis flax

**HABITAT** Open slopes, forest openings, meadows, disturbed areas, lowland to alpine

**BLOOMS** Spring, summer

**DESCRIPTION** Subshrub or herbaceous perennial, nonhairy, taprooted, stems several, erect, flowers in an open leafy cluster near the stem tip, plants 6–30 in. tall

**FLOWERS** Saucer-shaped, sepals 5, oval, petals 5, light to deep blue, sometimes white, wedge- to egg-shaped, ¼–1 in. long, stamens 5, styles 5, all the same length

**LEAVES** Alternate, not stalked, blades linear to lance-shaped, ¼–1 in. long, edges smooth, tips pointed or rounded

**FRUIT** Capsule, egg-shaped to round, seeds 10 or fewer

Willowy and graceful, wild blue flax plants bloom for about 6 weeks. Its seeds adhere readily to bare soil as they become sticky when moistened, aiding germination on burned sites and otherwise disturbed areas. Blue garden flax (*L. perenne*), a nonnative Eurasian species, is similar in appearance to wild blue flax, but has styles of 2 lengths.

Orobanchaceae—broomrape family
*Aphyllon purpureum* (*Orobanche uniflora*, *Aphyllon uniflorum*)

# naked broomrape, one-flowered broomrape

**HABITAT** Seeps, mossy crevices and ledges, bluffs, meadows, lowland to mid-montane

**BLOOMS** Spring

**DESCRIPTION** Annual or short-lived perennial, parasitic, glandular-hairy, nonphotosynthetic, stems short, leaves bractlike, the inflorescence one to several flowers, each single on a brownish stalk, plants 2–6 in. tall

**FLOWERS** Two-lipped, bluish purple, yellow, or creamy white, petal lobes 5, the edges fringed with hair, folds inside the floral tube bright yellow, sepals 5, linear with pointed tips

**LEAVES** Bractlike, lance-shaped, tips pointed

**FRUIT** Capsule, seeds many

Naked broomrape is known to be parasitic on sedums (*Sedum* spp.), saxifrages (*Saxifraga* spp.), members of the aster family, and other plants. It was long included within the *Orobanche* genus but was moved to *Aphyllon* along with other North and South American broomrape species based on DNA analysis that indicated they were different from Eurasian *Orobanche* species.

Plantaginaceae—plantain family
*Collinsia parviflora*

# small-flowered blue-eyed Mary





**HABITAT** Balds, meadows, rock outcrops, forest openings, lowland to alpine

**BLOOMS** Spring, summer

**DESCRIPTION** Annual, taprooted, stems erect, flowers solitary to several from the leaf axils, plants 1½–16 in. tall

**FLOWERS** Two-lipped, to ¼ in. long, sepal lobes 5, petal tube bent at 45 degrees near the base, lower lip dark blue to purplish, upper lip bluish white, pink, or white, stamens 4, pistil 1

**LEAVES** Opposite, sometimes in whorls of 3 near the stem tip, blades oval to linear, ¼–1½ in. long, tips pointed

**FRUIT** Capsule, oval, seeds 2–4

Small-flowered blue-eyed Mary thrives in thin-soiled areas within a variety of habitats and blooms early in the growing season while soils are moist. It is pollinated by bees and self-pollinates as well, a trait that maximizes seed set. Large-flowered blue-eyed Mary (*C. grandiflora*) is similar in appearance but has larger flowers and a petal tube bent at 90 degrees near the base.

Plantaginaceae—plantain family
*Penstemon fruticosus*

# shrubby penstemon





**HABITAT** Rock outcrops, forest openings, lower montane to alpine

**BLOOMS** Spring, summer

**DESCRIPTION** Shrub, clump-forming, stems few to many, upright, hairy or not, branched, flowers stalked, 1 to several at the stem tip and leaf axils, plants 6–16 in. tall

**FLOWERS** Two-lipped, lavender, blue, or purplish, 1–2 in. long, sepals 5-lobed, glandular-hairy, upper lip 2-lobed, lower lip 3-lobed and hairy inside, stamens 5, 1 sterile, anthers woolly-hairy

**LEAVES** Opposite along the stem, evergreen, blades linear to lance-shaped, ¼–2 in. long, edges smooth or toothed, tips pointed

**FRUIT** Capsule, seeds many

Penstemons have 4 fertile stamens and 1 sterile stamen called the staminode. Studies have shown that the staminode increases pollen transfer to the stigma. It can act as a lever to promote contact between pollinator and stigma or restrict nectar access, causing the bee to move around inside the flower, increasing pollen deposition. Staminode function varies among species and with bee size.

Plantaginaceae—plantain family
*Penstemon gairdneri*

# Gairdner's penstemon, Gairdner's beardtongue

**HABITAT** Shrub-steppe, rock areas, lowland to middle elevations

**BLOOMS** Spring

**DESCRIPTION** Subshrub, clump-forming, taprooted, stems few to many, erect, flowers solitary or few from the leaf axils, plants 4–16 in. tall

**FLOWERS** Two-lipped, ½–¾ in. long, lavender, blue, or rose, sepals 5-lobed, lance- to egg-shaped, petal tube narrow, upper lip 2-lobed, lower lip 3-lobed, glandular-hairy inside, stamens 5, 1 sterile

**LEAVES** Basal, stem leaves alternate or opposite, stalked or not, blades linear to spoon-shaped, surfaces short grayish-hairy, tips pointed

**FRUIT** Capsule, nonhairy, seeds many

Gairdner's penstemon grows in dry habitats with a thin soil layer. It has two varieties: var. *gairdneri* with alternate leaves and var. *oreganus* with opposite leaves. The genus name *Penstemon* comes from the words *pen* meaning "almost" and *stemon* meaning "a thread." Combined it means "almost a fertile stamen" a reference to the sterile stamen (staminode) common to all penstemon species.

Plantaginaceae—plantain family
*Penstemon speciosus*

# showy penstemon, royal penstemon

**HABITAT** Shrub-steppe, rocky areas, forest openings, low to high elevations

**BLOOMS** Spring, summer

**DESCRIPTION** Herbaceous perennial, taproot short with many thin, fibrous roots, stems several, stout, erect to spreading, flowers stalked, in a 1-sided cluster or in whorled tiers, plants 3–36 in. tall

**FLOWERS** Two-lipped, 1–1½ in. long, deep blue, pinkish blue, or violet, sepals 5-lobed, petal tube funnel-shaped, upper lip 2-lobed, lower lip 3-lobed with a white patch inside, stamens mostly nonhairy

**LEAVES** Basal and opposite along the stem, 1–3½ in. long, blades linear, oval, or spoon-shaped, surfaces hairy or not, edges smooth, tips rounded or pointed

**FRUIT** Capsule, egg-shaped, seeds many

Showy penstemon is a short-lived perennial found in dry habitats and disturbed areas. It grows on roadcuts, can resprout following fire, and reseeds readily. However, studies indicate that it is negatively impacted by the presence of cheatgrass (*Bromus tectorum*), showing reduced biomass and growth rates, likely due to resource competition.

Polemoniaceae—phlox family
*Polemonium occidentale*

## western polemonium, western Jacob's ladder

**HABITAT** Wet meadows, streambanks, fens, mid-montane to subalpine

**BLOOMS** Summer

**DESCRIPTION** Herbaceous perennial, glandular-hairy, rhizomatous, stem 1, erect, flowers in open, branched clusters near stem tips, plants 8–36 in. tall

**FLOWERS** Bell-shaped, to ½ in. long, stalked, sepals 5-lobed, lobes triangular, petal tube 5-lobed, sky blue to bluish purple with a white eye near the base, lobes egg-shaped, tips pointed, stamens 5, style 1

**LEAVES** Alternate along the stem and basal, 2–16 in. long, stalked, blades pinnately divided into 11–27 lance-shaped leaflets, tips pointed

**FRUIT** Capsule

Western polemonium is a tall, showy plant that usually grows among grasses, sedges, and forbs in wet habitats. It is pollinated by bumblebees and the leaves have a somewhat skunky odor when bruised. Similar species California sky-pilot (*P. californicum*) can be distinguished from western polemonium by its shorter stature, bell-shaped flowers with a yellow, rather than white, eye, and as it grows in shady forests rather than wetlands.

Ranunculaceae—buttercup family
*Aconitum columbianum*

# monkshood, Columbia monkshood





**HABITAT** Streambanks, wet meadows, forest openings, montane to subalpine

**BLOOMS** Summer

**DESCRIPTION** Herbaceous perennial, toxic, root tuberous, stems several, erect, inflorescence a narrow cluster of stalked flowers at the stem tips, plants 1½–6½ ft. tall

**FLOWERS** Hoodlike, glandular-hairy, sepals 5, deep bluish purple, occasionally white or cream, hoodlike upper sepal ¼–1 in. long, petals 2, inconspicuous, stamens many

**LEAVES** Alternate, those on the lower stem stalked, the upper stalkless, blade 2–7⅔ in. wide, divided into 3–5 lobes, lobes egg- to diamond-shaped, edges toothed to smooth, tips pointed

**FRUIT** Pod, 3–5 per flower, ¼–⅔ in. long, glandular-hairy or nonhairy, seeds ⅛ in. long

All parts of monkshood plants are considered toxic. Howell's aconite (*A. columbianum* ssp. *viviparum*), found in mid-montane habitats in Oregon and reportedly in Washington, forms bulblets in leaf axils and the inflorescence. Bulblets are a form of vegetative reproduction, plantlets that can grow into a new plant.

Ranunculaceae—buttercup family
*Anemone oregana*

## western wood anemone, Oregon anemone

**HABITAT** Forest openings, coastal bogs and marshes, lowland to mid-montane

**BLOOMS** Spring, summer

**DESCRIPTION** Herbaceous perennial, hairy, rhizomatous, stem 1, erect, flowers solitary at the stem tip, plants 4–12 in. tall

**FLOWERS** Saucer-shaped, petals absent, sepals usually 5, showy, oblong to egg-shaped, ¼–¾ in. long, blue to purplish, sometimes white or pink, or white above and reddish purple below, stamens more than 30

**LEAVES** Basal and whorled on the stem, stalked, blades palmately divided into 3 leaflets, leaflets lobed and partly toothed, to 3 in. long, tips pointed, stem leafless except for a whorl of 3 leaves just below flower

**FRUIT** Achene, hairy

Western wood anemone has two varieties: var. *oregana*, which grows in forests and has sepals of one color, and var. *felix* (inset), which is found in bogs and marshes near the coast an d has sepals that are white above and reddish purple below.

Ranunculaceae—buttercup family
*Clematis occidentalis*

# virgin's bower, Columbia clematis, rock clematis





**HABITAT** Forest openings, talus slopes, rock outcrops, shrub thickets, mid-montane to subalpine

**BLOOMS** Spring, summer

**DESCRIPTION** Perennial vine, hairy, rhizomatous, stems several, climbing or trailing, to 10 ft. long, flowers solitary from the leaf axils, nodding on stalks

**FLOWERS** Bell-shaped, sepals 4, showy, egg-shaped, blue, reddish purple, or violet, flaring outward as the flower opens, edges smooth, tips pointed, petals absent, stamens and pistils many

**LEAVES** Opposite, stalked, divided into 3 leaflets, leaflets triangular to egg-shaped, 1–4 in. long, edges toothed, lobed, or smooth, tips pointed

**FRUIT** Achene, hairy, topped with a feathery style

Virgin's bower has several varieties, with one, Columbia clematis (*C. occidentalis* var. *dissecta*), endemic to the Wenatchee Mountains area of Washington. Columbia clematis has reddish purple flowers, leaves with 1 or more lobed leaflets, and it often lacks a viny habit. In the rest of the western United States, virgin's bower is variety *grosseserrata*, which has blue to violet flowers and climbs vigorously.

Ranunculaceae—buttercup family
*Delphinium nuttallianum*

# upland larkspur, two-lobe larkspur, Nuttall's larkspur

**HABITAT** Shrub-steppe, dry forests, open slopes, lowland to mid-montane

**BLOOMS** Spring, summer

**DESCRIPTION** Herbaceous perennial, toxic, hairy or not, roots tuberous, stem 1, erect, mostly unbranched, inflorescence a narrow cluster of stalked flowers near the stem tip, plants 6–15½ in. tall

**FLOWERS** Spurred, sepals 5, showy, deep blue to bluish purple, rarely white, lobes oval to egg-shaped, tips rounded or pointed, spur ½–1 in. long, petals 4, the lower 2 deeply lobed, white to blue, rarely yellowish, stamens many, pistils 3

**LEAVES** Basal and alternate along the stem, stalked, blades round, divided into several leaflets or lobed, segments oblong to linear

**FRUIT** Pod, 3 per flower, seeds several

Upland larkspur is widespread and common in drier habitats. It is pollinated by bees, butterflies, and hummingbirds attracted by the nectar located in the long spur. All parts of upland larkspur are considered toxic to livestock and humans.

Violaceae—violet family
*Viola adunca*

## early blue violet, hooked violet, western dog violet

**HABITAT** Meadows, forest openings, streambanks, seeps, lowland to subalpine

**BLOOMS** Spring, summer

**DESCRIPTION** Herbaceous perennial, rhizomatous, stems many, flowers solitary on stalks from the leaf axils, plants mostly less than 5 in. tall

**FLOWERS** Spurred, petals 5, deep blue, violet, or lavender, spur slender, often curved, half as long as the petal blades, the side petals hairy at the base, the lowest one purple-lined, stamens 5, style tip hairy

**LEAVES** Alternate along the stem and basal, stalked, blades heart- to egg-shaped, ¼–1 in. long, edges round-toothed, tips rounded

**FRUIT** Capsule, oval, seeds several

A widely distributed species, early blue violet is a larval host for several rare butterflies. Early blue violet and many other *Viola* spp. produce cleistogamous, or closed, flowers. Cleistogamous flowers are self-pollinating and resemble buds. Having both types of flowers benefits the species by ensuring seed production while retaining the adaptability conferred by genetic exchange.

Violaceae—violet family
*Viola trinervata*

## sagebrush violet, three-nerved violet

**HABITAT** Shrub-steppe, rocky slopes, lowland to middle elevations

**BLOOMS** Spring

**DESCRIPTION** Herbaceous perennial, nonhairy, roots fibrous, stems several, erect to trailing, flowers solitary on stalks from the leaf axils, plants 2–6 in. tall

**FLOWERS** Spurred, spur short, petals 5, upper 2 petals dark reddish violet, lower 3 petals lilac or white with yellow at the base, brown-lined, stamens 5, style hairy at the tip

**LEAVES** Basal and alternate along the stem, grayish green, nonhairy, stalked, blades ¼–2 in. long, lobed or divided, leaflets or lobes oval

**FRUIT** Capsule, nonhairy, seeds tan

Sagebrush violet grows in lithosol shrub-steppe and other rocky areas. Unlike many violets, it does not have cleistogamous (closed) flowers. Sagebrush violet capsules contract as they open, catapulting the seed away from the parent plant. Similar species Beckwith's violet (*V. beckwithii*), present in Oregon but not in Washington, can be distinguished by its hairy leaves with linear, rather than oval, lobes.

# Green and Brown Flowers

Apiaceae—parsley family
*Lomatium dissectum*

# fern-leaved desert parsley, chocolate tips

**HABITAT** Talus slopes, dry forest openings, shrub-steppe, streambanks, lowland to mid-montane

**BLOOMS** Spring

**DESCRIPTION** Aromatic herbaceous perennial, taprooted, stems several, upright, nonhairy, leaves fernlike, inflorescence umbrella-shaped, rays of the umbel 1–4 in. long, each ray with a flower cluster at the tip, plants 1½–5 ft. tall

**FLOWERS** Tiny, sepals absent, petals 5, purplish brown or yellow, stamens 5, styles 2, flowers bisexual or male only

**LEAVES** Basal and alternate along the stem, stalked, blades divided into linear leaflets, leaflet edges lobed, stem leaves similar but smaller and stalkless

**FRUIT** Dry, oval with a thickened edge, 2-seeded

Fern-leaved desert parsley is long-lived and has a thick taproot up to 2 feet long. Although its flowers are visited by many types of insects, studies show bees are key to successful pollination. Fern-leaved desert parsley is fire tolerant, resprouting from the root crown post-fire. It is often utilized in dryland restoration efforts.

Orchidaceae—orchid family
*Platanthera stricta (Habenaria saccata)*

# slender bog orchid, male habenaria

**HABITAT** Wet meadows, seeps, streambanks, lowland to subalpine

**BLOOMS** Summer

**DESCRIPTION** Herbaceous perennial, nonhairy, roots fibrous, stem slender, erect, inflorescence an open, leafy-bracted cluster at the stem tip, flowers fragrant but not showy, plants 6–36 in. tall

**FLOWERS** Hoodlike, green to yellowish green, sepals 3, the upper sepal forming part of the hood, petals 3, 2 petals curved upward, the 3rd liplike, lance-shaped, with a sac-shaped spur at the base, spur half to two-thirds as long as the lip

**LEAVES** Alternate, nonhairy, 1–6 in. long, blades egg- to lance-shaped, leaf tips rounded or pointed

**FRUIT** Capsule, oval, seeds many

Orchids have developed an effective way to transfer large quantities of pollen from one flower to another. They have structures called pollinaria that consist of 2 stalked pollen sacs connected at a sticky base. The sticky base can attach the pollinarium to visiting insects, who then unwittingly carry it to the next flower distributing the pollen.

# GOING FURTHER



This book is just an introduction to the wonders of Pacific Northwest native plants, profiling 150 of the showiest and most common wildflowers. We hope we've piqued your interest, and you'll continue exploring and learning about our native flora. There are a LOT of plants to discover here. There are about 3700 taxa in Washington with 2662 considered native and about 5500 taxa in Oregon with 4140 natives. The term "taxa" includes species plus their subspecies and varieties. These plants include what we usually think of as wildflowers, plus trees, shrubs, grasses and grasslike plants, ferns, and aquatics.

You could easily spend a lifetime studying our native flora and never see and learn all the plants. We have each dedicated decades to traveling around our region exploring for plants. Each year we encounter plants that are new to us as we travel to places that we hadn't previously visited. As you further your study of our flora, you'll want to consult other more comprehensive books and make use of online references. Here are some of our favorites that we consult.

## Books: Field Guides

We're a bit prejudiced, but these comprehensive books from Timber Press have sold thousands of copies and have become dog-eared and well used by plant lovers throughout the Northwest:

- *Wildflowers of the Pacific Northwest*, Mark Turner and Phyllis Gustafson, 2006.

- *Trees and Shrubs of the Pacific Northwest*, Mark Turner and Ellen Kuhlmann, 2014.
- *Weeds of the Pacific Northwest*, Mark Turner and Sami Gray, 2024.





If you're looking for more of a natural history approach in a book that includes plants, animals, fungi, geology, and climate we recommend another book published by Timber Press: *Natural History of the Pacific Northwest Mountains*, Daniel Mathews, 2017.

Along with many of our plant-loving friends, we often carry one of these books from Lone Pine Publishing when we're out in the field. These volumes include a bit of ethnobotany for many of the plants they cover:

- *Plants of the Pacific Northwest Coast*, Jim Pojar and Andy MacKinnon, 2016.
- *Plants of Southern Interior British Columbia and the Inland Northwest*, Roberta Parish, Ray Coupé, and Dennis Lloyd, 1996.
- *Alpine Plants of the Northwest, Wyoming to Alaska,* Jim Pojar and Andy MacKinnon, 2013.
- *Wild Berries of Washington and Oregon*, T. Abe Lloyd and Fiona Hamersley Chambers, 2014.

## Books: Technical References

Botanical technical references can be intimidating, even for experienced users. It takes time and practice to learn to use a dichotomous key as you carefully examine often obscure details of a plant. You'll likely make good use of your hand lens as you hone your observation skills. But these books are the standard references used by professional botanists (and field guide authors):

- *Flora of the Pacific Northwest: An Illustrated Manual*. Second Edition. C. Leo Hitchcock and Arthur Cronquist, edited by David E. Giblin, Ben S. Legler, Peter F. Zika, and Richard G. Olmstead. University of Washington Press, 2018.
- *Vascular Plants of the Pacific Northwest*. C. Leo Hitchcock, Arthur Cronquist, Marion Ownbey, and J. W. Thompson. Five volumes. University of Washington Press, 1955–1969.
- *Flora of Oregon*. Stephen C. Meyers, Thea Jaster, Katie E. Mitchell, Linda K. Hardison. Three volumes. Botanical Research Institute of Texas Press, 2015-2025.

If you're on the northern or southern edge of our territory, the technical manuals for British Columbia and California can be useful:

- *Illustrated Flora of British Columbia*. G. W. Douglas, et al., editors. Eight volumes. Crown Publishers, King's Printer for British Columbia, 1998–2002.
- *The Jepson Manual: Vascular Plants of California*. Bruce G. Baldwin, et al., editors. University of California Press, 2012.

## Smartphone Apps

Books can get heavy in your pack and you probably carry a smartphone with you most of the time. While we haven't gotten to the point of having a plug-in DNA analyzer for our phones, these first two apps can substitute for a field guide. They include simplified keys, multiple photos for most plants, descriptive text, and distribution maps. Both of these are self-contained and once downloaded do not require an internet connection:





- *Oregon WildFlowers: A Guide to the Wildflowers, Shrubs, and Vines of Oregon*. Oregon Flora Project, Botany and Plant Pathology Department, Oregon State University, and High Country Apps, LLC. 2014 (and regularly updated).
- *Washington WildFlowers: A Guide to the Wildflowers, Shrubs, and Vines of Washington and Surrounding Areas*. University of Washington, Burke Museum, and High Country Apps, LLC. 2013 (and regularly updated).

Many people are looking for the easy way out: an app that will identify a plant just from a picture. While this technology is getting better each year, it's still prone to making incorrect identifications. Sometimes they get it right and sometimes they don't. You'll probably want to confirm what an auto-identification app is suggesting by consulting another source if you're concerned about accuracy.

- Apple's *Visual Look Up*, in iOS 15 or later on iPhones and newer iPads, uses Siri to attempt to identify plants, dog breeds, and landmarks. It needs an internet connection and doesn't work with all photos.

- *Google Lens* is in the camera app of select Android devices and is also available to download for other Android devices and iPhones. It requires an internet connection to work.
- *iNaturalist* is much more than just an app. It's available for Apple and Android, as well as the web browser on your laptop or desktop computer. To use it, you upload one or more photos of a plant (or other organism), and the software attempts to identify it based on thousands of other photos that have been identified by experts. Photos you upload are added to the database, contributing to citizen science worldwide. You can also use iNaturalist to search for specific plants and see where they've been found by other users.
- *Seek by iNaturalist* identifies plants, wildlife, and fungi. This app, available for Android and Apple, draws on observations submitted to iNaturalist.org and partner sites, and identified by the iNaturalist community. It requires an internet connection to work.

## Websites

Websites can be a better source of up-to-date information about plants, particularly currently accepted names, since they can be updated relatively easily and frequently compared to books that are expensive and time-consuming to revise and print. Most of the websites we suggest include plant photos as well as current taxonomic details.

- **Burke Herbarium Image Collection:** burkeherbarium.org/imagecollection. Developed and maintained by the University of Washington Herbarium at the Burke Museum, the site has over 3200 vascular plant species with photos. It includes a simplified key as well as several ways to search the collection.



- **OregonFlora:** oregonflora.org. OregonFlora is based at the OSU Herbarium at Oregon State University. The site is comprehensive for Oregon's plants and includes simplified keys, search functions, and a mapping tool to identify plants found within an area.
- **CalFlora:** calflora.org. CalFlora is run by a nonprofit set up to provide the service, which includes data and photos for all of California's flora (some of which is also found in Oregon and Washington), along with extensive search and mapping tools. CalFlora links to CalPhotos (calphotos.berkeley.edu), a collection of about 800,000 photos (and growing) of plants, animals, fossils, people, and landscapes from around the world.
- **E-Flora BC (Electronic Atlas of the Flora of British Columbia):** linnet.geog.ubc.ca/biodiversity/eflora. E-Flora BC comes from the University of British Columbia. It includes all the plants considered to be part of the flora of British Columbia and some plants from adjacent areas. Included are species descriptions and illustrations from the eight-volume Illustrated *Flora of British Columbia* and interactive maps showing where the species have been found.
- **Pacific Northwest Wildflowers:** pnwflowers.com. This website from Mark Turner, one of the authors of this book and three other printed field guides, houses a collection of over 16,000 plant photos and a searchable

database that accesses the descriptions and distribution maps from *Wildflowers of the Pacific Northwest*.



- **Flora of North America:** floranorthamerica.org. This site is the online version of the thirty-volume *Flora of North America* and includes all the text from those volumes as well as some updates since the books were printed. You can browse by family or genus or search for a plant if you know its name.
- **USDA PLANTS Database:** plants.sc.egov.usda.gov/home. The PLANTS Database provides standardized information about the vascular plants, mosses, liverworts, hornworts, and lichens of the United States and its territories. It's searchable in several ways and maps plant distributions by state (and in some cases, by county).
- **Plants of the World Online (POWO):** powo.science.kew.org. This site, from the Royal Botanical Gardens, Kew, is a great resource for finding the currently accepted name for a plant. It includes some photos and maps distribution at the state or provincial level.
- **Ecoregions of North America:** epa.gov/eco-research/ecoregions-north-america. This is the site from which we drew the information in the ecoregions section of the climate and habitat chapter of this book.

There are many other websites dedicated to plant identification, but the ones we've listed are the ones we consult routinely when we find a plant new to us or want to check distribution data.

# GLOSSARY



**achene.** Small, dry fruit, containing one seed.

**alkaloids.** Water-insoluble, nitrogen-containing compounds that often exhibit pharmacological action, such as nicotine.

**alpine.** Found above timberline at high altitude.

**alternate.** Arranged singly at different heights along the stem.

**annual.** Plant that germinates, flowers, sets seed, and dies in one year.

**anther.** Pollen-producing segment of the stamen.

**appressed.** Lying flat against another organ, as hairs pressed against the surface of a leaf or stem.

**aquatic.** Growing in or on water, floating or rooted to soil at the bottom with submerged stems or shoots.

**ascending.** Curving or angling upward from the base.

**axil.** The upper angle between the leaf and the stem.

**basal.** Found at or near the base of a plant or plant part.

**berry.** Fleshy fruit with more than one seed within the soft tissue.

**biennial.** Plant completing its life cycle in two years.

**bisexual.** Having functional male and female reproductive structures.

**blade.** The expanded part of the leaf.

**bract.** Leaflike structure, usually associated with the inflorescence, but also sometimes on the stem.

**branch.** Secondary stem, growing from main stem.

**bristle.** 1. Large stiff straight hair. 2. Aster family, fine hairs at top of flower arising from inferior ovary.

**bulb.** An underground bud, enlarged for nutritive storage from which stems and roots are formed.

**bulblet.** A small bulb, associated with the root or stem system.

**capsule.** Dry, many-seeded fruit.

**caudex.** Persistent base of an herbaceous perennial.

**circumboreal.** Located or distributed around the world at northern latitudes.

**deciduous.** Quality or characteristic of something being shed or discarded seasonally.

**disk.** In the aster family, the part of the head made up of disk flowers.

**disk flower.** Flower in the aster family with a regular, tubular shape, rayless.

**egg-shaped.** Leaf blade wider on one end and narrower at the other.

**elaiosome.** Fleshy structure attached to the outside of a seed.

**endemic.** Limited to a certain geographic or edaphic area.

**ephemeral.** Lasting for a short period of time.

**erect.** Upright from the ground.

**evergreen.** Living through one or more cycle of seasons, as in evergreen leaves. *See also* deciduous.

**extirpated.** No longer in existence in a particular region, but still living in other areas of the world.

**fibrous root.** Type of root system with all root branches the same width or thickness.

**fleshy.** Thick, juicy, as in many plants in the sedum family.

**fruit.** Any ripened ovary and associated structures containing the seed(s).

**fused.** United, as petals to sepals or petals, sepals to each other, not free.

**genus.** Taxonomic rank smaller than a family and greater than the species level. Plural genera.

**glabrous.** Smooth, without hairs.

**gland.** Small, round body that emits a sticky substance, sessile on outer plant surface or on end of a hair.

**hair.** Thin to thick threadlike growth on outer surface.

**head.** Dense collection of sessile or nearly sessile flowers making up the inflorescence. Often said of members of the aster family.

**hybrid.** Plant created when two different species interbreed.

**inflorescence.** The arrangement of the flowers, or cluster of flowers of a plant.

**leaflet.** Portion of a divided or compound leaf blade.

**linear.** Narrow with parallel sides.

**lip.** Upper or lower section of an unequal corolla or calyx.

**lithosol.** Type of shallow soil with hard rock underneath.

**lobe.** A subdivided segment of an organ. The free parts of a flower tube.

**native.** Growing in place without human aid or actions.

**nut.** A hard, dry fruit containing a single seed.

**nutlet.** Small fruit, looks like a nut, usually one of several.

**oblong.** Longer than wide, rounded.

**opposite.** Arranged in pairs at same level, and on opposite sides, often said of leaves on the stem.

**oval.** An ellipse.

**ovary.** The organ that contains the ovules, usually develops into the fruit after fertilization. The wide portion of the pistil.

**palmate.** Divided from a single point and radiating around it.

**parasite.** Plant that receives part or all of its nutrition from another organism.

**perennial.** Plant living longer than two years.

**persistent.** Remaining attached, not falling off plant for some time.

**petal.** Member or segment of the corolla, the inner perianth whorl, often colored.

**pinnate.** Divided into leaflets arranged on opposite sides of an axis.

**pistil.** Female reproductive organ of a plant, usually consisting of an ovary, style, and stigma.

**prickle.** A sharp growth, thorn, or spine, usually restricted to smaller growths.

**ray.** Strap-shaped petal of a flower in the aster family or a stalk of an umbel inflorescence.

**ray flower.** Aster family flower with one long strap-shaped petal, often with three lobes.

**rhizomatous.** Plant that has rhizomes.

**rhizome.** A horizontal stem below the ground that sends off rootlets and vertical stems or leaves.

**root.** Structure from base of stem, usually underground. Anchors the plant and absorbs minerals and water.

**root crown.** Area of root where the stems are formed.

**rosette.** Cluster of leaves at ground level, usually in a circle.

**seed.** Plant embryo, usually packaged with starchy, nutritive tissue and surrounded by a protective coating.

**sepal.** A fused or free member of the calyx, usually green and bractlike.

**serpentine.** Common term for rock or soil high in magnesium and heavy metals such as chromium and nickel and low in calcium. Often has specialized flora.

**shrub.** Woody plant that usually has several main stems, or is branched from the base.

**spine.** Stiff, slender, sharply pointed structure.

**spreading.** Held outward from point of attachment.

**spur.** Hollow, usually rounded projection from petal or sepal, containing nectar.

**stalk.** Secondary stem, often referring to structure supporting a flower or leaf blade.

**stamen.** Male reproductive organ bearing pollen composed of a stalk (filament) and pollen sacs (anther).

**staminode.** Modified stamen that does not produce pollen.

**stem.** The central support of a plant bearing the other organs, such as leaves and flowers, usually aboveground.

**stigma.** Part of the pistil where pollen may attach.

**stipule.** Appendage at base of a leafstalk, generally paired, variable in form, often leaflike, sometimes scalelike or a spine.

**stolon.** Runner, an elongated stem lying on the ground, forms new roots and stems.

**stoloniferous.** Plant that has stolons.

**style.** Usually slender portion of the pistil connecting the ovary and the stigma.

**subalpine.** Just below timberline.

**subshrub.** Plant with woody tissue only near the base of stems and in the root system.

**talus.** Mass of medium- to large-sized rock fragments at the base of a cliff.

**taproot.** A larger main root from which smaller root branches are formed.

**teeth.** Alternating projections and indentations on the margin or edge.

**tendril.** Slender twining or coiling structure, by which a climbing plant grasps for support.

**tepal.** An undifferentiated petal and/or sepal, in which sepals and petals look the same.

**throat.** The expanded opening of flowers with fused sepals or petals.

**tube.** Fused sepals or petals forming a cylindrical structure.

**tuft.** Cluster of something such as hair, leaves, or flowers growing from a common point.

**umbel.** Inflorescence with three or more stalks radiating from a common point.

**unisexual.** Having either male or female reproductive structures.

**vein.** Vessels by which water and nutrients are transported. Often easily seen in leaves.

**vernal.** Pertaining to spring.

**vine.** Trailing or climbing plant with a long, flexible stem and often supporting itself by use of tendrils.

# INDEX

© Brian Turner

**Mark Turner** has more than thirty years of experience photographing garden and native plants for books and magazines. He brings the eye of an artist together with the mind of a botanist to create clear, high-content photographs that enable viewers to learn about and understand the characteristics of the plants he photographs. Mark is a past board member of the Washington Native Plant Society and maintains a website about Pacific Northwest wildflowers (pnwflowers.com). He is also a well-regarded speaker on the garden club and native plant circuit and gives workshops on both plants and photography. Mark lives in Bellingham, Washington.

© Mark Turner

**Ellen Kuhlmann** is a professional botanist with extensive experience with Northwest flora. She has a background in fire ecology, rare plant research, and plant community ecology. She worked for the US Forest Service for many years, and for six years was the project manager for Seeds of Success, Washington Rare Plant Care and Conservation (Rare Care), a program sponsored by the Royal Botanic Gardens, Kew. Ellen lives in Bellingham, Washington.